THE
LEADING
LADY

By Betty White

Betty White in Person
Betty White's Pet Love: How Pets Take Care of Us
  (with Thomas J. Watson)

By Tom Sullivan

If You Could See What I Hear (with Derek Gill)
Adventures in Darkness (with Derek Gill)
Common Senses
You Are Special

THE READING LADY

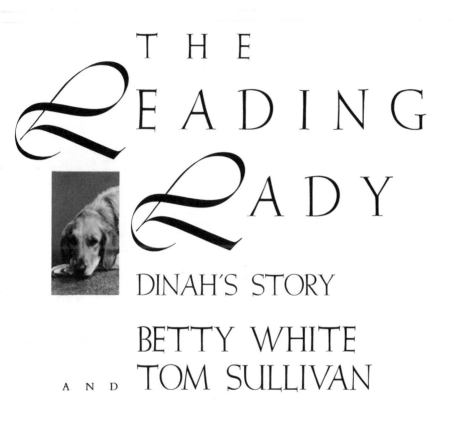

DINAH'S STORY

BETTY WHITE

A N D TOM SULLIVAN

BANTAM BOOKS
NEW YORK • TORONTO • LONDON • SYDNEY • AUCKLAND

Grateful acknowledgment is made for permission to reprint the following
(which appears on p. vii):

"To Know the Dark" from *Farming: A Hand Book,* copyright © 1967 by
Wendell Berry, reprinted by permission of Harcourt Brace Jovanovich, Inc.

THE LEADING LADY: DINAH'S STORY

A Bantam Book / October 1991

Library of Congress Cataloging-in-Publication Data
White, Betty, 1924–
    The leading lady : Dinah's story / Betty White and Tom Sullivan.
      p.   cm.
    ISBN 0-553-07395-8
    1. Dinah (Dog)   2. Guide dogs—United States—Biography.
3. Sullivan, Tom, 1947– .   4. Blind musicians—United States—
Biography.   I. Sullivan, Tom, 1947– .   II. Title.
HV1780.W48   1991
636.7'0886—dc20   91-11981
                                                              CIP

Published simultaneously in the United States and Canada

Bantam Books are published by Bantam Books, a division of Bantam Double-
day Dell Publishing Group, Inc. Its trademark, consisting of the words
"Bantam Books" and the portrayal of a rooster, is Registered in U.S. Patent
and Trademark Office and in other countries. Marca Registrada. Bantam
Books, 666 Fifth Avenue, New York, New York 10103.

PRINTED IN THE UNITED STATES OF AMERICA
RRH   0 9 8 7 6 5 4 3 2 1

To the Lady herself—for whom the word *dedication* could have been invented

To go in the dark with a light is to know the light.
To know the dark, go dark. Go without sight,
and find that the dark, too, blooms and sings,
and is traveled by dark feet and dark wings.

From *Farming: A Hand Book*
by Wendell Berry

ACKNOWLEDGMENTS

Our warmest thanks must go to:

LORETTA BARRETT—our literary agent whose positive response to those first tentative pages provided fuel for the whole trip.

GENE YOUNG—our editor at Bantam who taught us to follow each other like parade elephants as we told our story.

HAROLD SMITH—for his love and expertise in bringing both Dinah and Nelson to fulfillment.

JENNIFER CONROY—and all the dedicated people at Guide Dogs for the Blind, not only for their hospitality and cooperation, but for all they continue to accomplish.

JERRY MARTIN—who was there when the idea was born and whose unfailing encouragement made the difference.

MARJORIE JUDGE—and her helpers at EDA Secretarial Services for all the typing as well as the enthusiastic interest.

MIKE DONALDSON—who blended equal measures of love and law.

LEADER DOGS—for allowing Smitty's time with me to be so flexible.

PATTY, BLYTHE & TOM—who have always loved as honestly as Dinah.

Plus the good friends kind enough to read a work in progress and make it such fun. You know who you are.

Love,

Betty and Tom

PROLOGUE

TOM SULLIVAN AND HIS FAMILY have been my treasured friends for some twenty plus years. Not too long ago, I would have said we all knew each other completely. However, it took one special golden retriever to bring a whole new dimension, not only to our friendship but to each of our lives.

The Leading Lady was not planned in advance. "You know, someday we should really write a book about this. . . ." There was none of that. One afternoon I was relaxing in my living room, enjoying a rambling conversation with a friend. As usual, Dinah was a participating third party, smiling from face to face as we visited—hers was just not a speaking part. Quite suddenly, I was struck by the realization that I was privileged to be part of something rather extraordinary that had to be documented.

Once the thought had fastened itself in my head, I couldn't jar it loose. I let it simmer for a few days. Then, during a phone conversation with Tom, I casually broached the subject of putting

Dinah's story down on paper. His instant response was an enthusiastic affirmative, and we were off and running.

Tom and I did not write this book "together." Tom wrote of *his* Dinah through the years and I wrote of the Dinah—and the Tom—that *I* know. We would exchange chapters as we went along, and because we both have ridiculously busy work schedules, we would often trade the pages by mail, touching base only now and then by phone.

Independently, we both found that Dinah took us into areas much farther afield than the original premise, but we had a very good time following where she led. This is by no means a "my favorite pet" book. This is the story of a world-class working animal; of her outreach and her influence on the lives of her friends. It is also the story of those friends.

Betty White
Carmel, California

ACT ONE

1

BETTY

ASKING PEOPLE TO MY house for dinner is not my best thing. Much as I enjoy having them there, I am neither a secure hostess nor a comfortable one—this in spite of the fact that I have a lovely housekeeper, Edna McNair, who does all the hard part. Even if there's only going to be one couple, I am still a worrier, unable to relax until my guests arrive.

Perhaps I'm not the only one who feels this way, but other people manage to make it look so easy that I am totally intimidated. As a result, the ones who get invited are usually cherished friends of long standing.

Tom and Patty Sullivan certainly fit that description, and in recent years we have managed to spend an evening together every few weeks. Indeed, they are such dear friends that they indulge my shortcomings, and when it is my turn they aren't insulted if I opt to take them out to dinner. On rare occasions, however, I shame myself into entertaining them at home—as was the case one special April evening in 1987.

While Edna was doing all the significant things, I attempted to get creative with hors d'oeuvres, trying to forget the fact that Patty is one of those miracle hostesses who graciously serves up a gourmet dinner for twelve with no help—other than a willing and beautiful daughter—without ever seeming to have left the room! She laughs when I accuse her of this. To her, it is par for the course.

I realized my only chance was to keep it simple. So, for one of the starters, I remembered an easy appetizer that I had seen Tom enjoy. I scored a couple of cucumbers with a fork, sliced them thick, spread on some light cream cheese, and added a dollop of caviar—the domestic kind, certainly not the expensive imported stuff. I mean, I love Tom a lot, but there is a limit! I used the black caviar on some of the slices and the red on others, which made it look very pretty. Tom wouldn't see it—he's been blind all his life—but he'd taste the difference and know I'd tried.

Tom Sullivan is well-known for any or all of a number of reasons: for his records, his books, his lectures, the music he has composed, the movies he has written and produced, and certainly for his performances on a great number of popular television shows. His autobiography, *If You Could See What I Hear,* was made into a feature motion picture. Tom's professional accomplishments are impressive, but he also surfs. He skis. He rides. He has made thirty-seven sky dives and is a 90's golfer as well as a long-distance marathon runner. He has even driven a motorcycle—fortunately not far. A stimulating friend, to say the least.

I went on fiddling with the appetizer plate, trying not to get in Edna's way, but I'm sure she wasn't sorry when the doorbell rang. Once the Sullivans arrived, my nerves evaporated and the party was on. The three of us always have so much to say to each other that we begin fighting for turns before the front door closes. Adding to the happy confusion, as always, were my two small dogs, Timothy and Cricket, who take on the co-hosting chores with inordinate enthusiasm.

As the first greetings more or less subsided and the drinks were mixed, we settled in the living room by the fire. Naturally, one of my first questions was "How is everybody?" I was assured that everybody was great.

"Everybody" in the Sullivan family, at that point in time, meant lovely Blythe, seventeen, and young Tom, better known as Sully, fifteen, as well as the four-legged members of the family. There was the star, Tom's golden retriever guide dog, Dinah, who was stepping into retirement; Cay, a German shepherd, who never reminds you of the fact that he holds a Schutzhund degree in protection; Season, a tiny Maltese terrier, who is convinced that *she* is the one with the degree; and, finally, the most recent addition to the family, Nelson, a strapping two-year-old black Labrador retriever, come to take over for Dinah as Tom's new leader dog.

For the past nine years, Dinah had been Tom's right arm as well as his eyes. She was well into "mature" by now, and though she was fine in every other respect, her eyes were beginning to cloud slightly. Not enough even to be noticed in any but a working dog. It was Tom, blind since birth, who was the first to become aware that Dinah's eyesight wasn't quite as sharp as it once was. He could feel her turn her head to get peripheral vision instead of meeting the world head on as she had always done.

Tom travels constantly on speaking engagements, often with Dinah as sole companion, and he finally had to admit she was losing her edge. She just wasn't as sure as she used to be. It had become apparent that her retirement was in order for the good of all concerned. As Tom told her, "You can take your girdle off and relax now, honey—you've earned it." So it was that on the night of our dinner Nelson had been the new kid on the block for almost three months.

It soon became abundantly clear to me that everybody was *not* great.

"It's Dinah." Tom shook his head in frustration. "She's a different dog. I've tried everything. She won't eat; she won't even come when I call her, so I know there is something very wrong."

Patty was equally concerned. "She won't even look at him."

"What's worse, she won't run on the beach with me"—Tom's voice broke—"and that was always her big treat! Betty, I don't know what to do!"

I knew this dog, and I couldn't imagine the unflappable Dinah, who had been part of Tom for all that time, being anything but anxious to please. "Are you sure she feels okay?"

"The vet checked her over completely. Even her eyes are no problem if she's not working. He told me it's like some men who are fine as long as they have a job to go to; then they retire, and *bang!* they fall apart. Don't laugh: that's what he said."

I didn't feel in the least like laughing.

Tom went on. "I always knew she'd retire someday, sure, even if I didn't like to think about it, but I just took it for granted she'd sit back and enjoy being part of the family without having to work. But she crawls under the bed and lies there all day, and you can just feel the waves of depression."

Reaching for Tom's hand, Patty said, "It isn't something we're imagining. It's heartbreaking to watch."

Not Dinah. They couldn't be talking about *Dinah*.

"I could take her back to Leader Dogs where I got her, and they'd give her fine care for the rest of her life, but Dinah—my Dinah—would be living in a kennel! Somebody would come by once or twice a day, say 'Good girl!' and leave. I couldn't stand that. Jesus, Betty, she's not quite twelve. She's got good time yet. What'll I *do*?"

There was a moment of silence before he continued.

"I don't know how to say it, because people are always hitting you with this, but is there anybody you might know who could maybe give her the attention she needs? We can't reach her. It's as though she feels that somebody came in and took her job and took her master and she can't handle it. She's trying to die."

There was another long moment. Finally, I heard a voice saying, "Would you like *me* to try her, Tom?"

The voice, I suddenly realized, was my own, but I had had nothing to do with the impulse. I already had two little dogs and a cat and an incredibly busy schedule and my life was in order.

Or so I had thought.

I was wrong.

It was the beginning of one of the happiest learning adventures of my life.

On occasion through the years, I have been known to shoot from the hip and have often lived to regret it. For the record, we were on about the second sip of our first drink, so this was not mere bottled enthusiasm. It was something that simply had to be.

Trying hard to be a grownup, I realized there were some major considerations that had to be addressed before taking on a new member of the family—all of which raced through my mind in that long beat after Tom finished speaking. How would my existing tribe take to a new addition? How would they get along?

Well, Dinah had lived with Season, the Maltese, from the beginning, so horsey little dogs were her cup of tea. She should do fine with my eight-year-old, Timothy, a very small miniature black poodle, who is a bundle of positive energy. Tim loves the world.

Then there was Cricket. By sheer luck, I had come upon this bar of soap–sized puppy at the Oakland SPCA when he was less than six weeks old; he was now almost four years and had stopped just short of growing into a fine Bichon Frisé. Crick is a shade smaller than Timmy but weighs in at nearly three times as much—not fat, just density. He is a little cream-colored lead balloon.

Finally, there was the black cat, T.K. ("Timmy's Kitty," since she had followed him into the house six years ago, and he was the only one of us she would tolerate for the first four years). T.K. no longer goes outside, but she lives such a symbiotic existence with us in the house I had no doubt that, if necessary, she could arrange to be where Dinah wasn't, at all times.

So the fateful words had been spoken: "Would you like me to try her, Tom?"

Once they were said, we all came undone, laughing and crying. Tom kept saying over and over that he had never expected or intended that *I* would volunteer. Whether true or not, it doesn't matter.

I called Edna in from her dinner preparation.

"Edna, how would you feel about having a beautiful, big, well-mannered lady dog come to live with us?" I explained the circumstances.

It so happened that for a long time Edna had been talking about how nice it would be to have a big dog along with the little ones. She had often allowed as how it would make her feel more secure when I was out of town—especially those times when I took the two little guys with me up to my place in Carmel. Consequently, I didn't look for much opposition from this quarter.

Sure enough, a slow smile spread over her face, and in her quiet, understated way, she simply said, "Why, I think we can do that."

It's a good thing Edna took this momentous decision quietly, because none of the rest of us did. What we had for dinner or how it was, I couldn't say. Maybe that's the solution to all my worrying beforehand. Give me a new dog and I won't care!

It wasn't quite as giddy as I make it sound in retrospect. There were some practical matters and some logistics to work out.

Above all, I wanted to give Tom and Patty plenty of chance to reconsider. They must talk with Blythe and Sully, both of whom were devoted to Dinah, and be very sure this was something everyone could handle.

It was agreed that we would all think it through, work out the details, and then, if it still seemed the right thing to do, the Sullivans would bring Dinah over in two weeks—on Easter Sunday, April 19.

We kissed good night, and maybe the hugs were just a little tighter than on other evenings. Patty and Tom headed for the car, Tom's hand, as usual, on Patty's shoulder, as they went down the steps. It is always done so naturally that I often literally forget the fact that Tom can't see.

As they got to the car, Tom reached for Patty's keys. "I'll drive home, honey."

He loves that joke. So do I.

I waved them on their way, closed the door, and just stood there for a moment. A lot had happened tonight.

It was amazing to realize how far we had all come together and how our friendship had grown over the years since we'd all first met on Cape Cod in 1968.

My husband, Allen Ludden, and I were doing a summer stock production of *Bell, Book, and Candle* at the Cape Playhouse in Dennis, Massachusetts. Every night, after the show, Allen and I would head for a little restaurant bar near the theater, the Deacon's Perch, to have a drink and a bowl of steamed clams and listen to a young blind singer who was performing there on his summer off from Harvard.

Young Tom Sullivan was full of himself and sang up a storm. Each night, as soon as he heard we had come in, he would immediately launch into our favorite tunes. He was a great fan of

Allen's *G.E. College Bowl* on television, as well as his game show, *Password*. It was sweet of Tom, if not too diplomatic, to say he had "watched me on TV as well—for *years!*"

Yes, although he has been blind all his life, Tom *watches* television and goes to *see* movies. Take my word for it, he gets more out of both than many of us with eyes. At first that used to amaze me, but through the years I have learned not to be surprised by anything this man can do.

Tom grew up using his lack of sight as a personal goad to conquer things most of his sighted friends found too difficult. He is not a show-off. He simply refuses to take a passive role in life. As he puts it, "My blindness isn't a handicap, it's one big hell of an inconvenience!"

Allen and I weren't the only ones who enjoyed Tom's singing. The Deacon's Perch was packed every night. This brash young man could put me away with his rendition of "By the Time I Get to Phoenix" (he still can). It was no wonder there was always a covey of young beauties hovering around, but the loveliest of them all, one Patty Steffan, stayed quietly in the background and bided her time.

It was never enough for my husband simply to enjoy Tom's kind of special performance and then move on. There was a touch of the entrepreneur in there somewhere. For whenever Allen saw a truly extraordinary young talent, he couldn't rest until he tried to make someone else aware of it as well. When we returned to New York after closing the play, he called Mike Douglas, who was doing his highly rated national variety show every day from Philadelphia, and per Allen's suggestion, Mike invited Tom to sing on his show.

Not surprisingly, the young Irishman was a smash and Tom's career began to take off, eventually bringing him to California. At that point, entrepreneur Ludden, classic Libra that he was, switched scales and began to lecture Tom on the value of finishing college.

That's where the friendship started. The difference in our ages never seemed to occur to us. How could that possibly have been twenty years ago?

As with all good friends, when circumstances kept us apart for long periods of time, maybe as much as a year or so at a stretch, the minute we got back together again we would pick up mid-sentence. Of course, Tom got smart very early on and married the dear and beautiful Patty. Ever since then, whenever Tom gets a little carried away, the standard put-down among his closest group of buddies has been, "Tom, if you don't shape up, we'll tell you what your wife *really* looks like."

I went to let Tim and Crick out for their good-night pit stop, still bemused by the unexpected turns life can take. Allen and I had known about it when Tom got his young Dinah from Leader Dogs. Allen was taken from us six years ago—and now that same Dinah was coming to me. That is, *maybe* Dinah was coming to me. I mustn't count on it. I had seen the pain on Tom's face, even while he was making his jokes. He may well have had second thoughts after he left. I turned out the lights and we all headed upstairs. The time had come to explain to T.K.

Later, as I drifted off to sleep, I found myself praying that Tom wouldn't have a change of heart on the way home.

2
TOM

PATTY DIDN'T GIVE ME the keys and I didn't drive home.
Why is it that I always make a joke at the worst possible
times? I'd like to think it's because I'm trying to make people
relax. In truth, it's probably because I'm having trouble coping
with an uncomfortable situation. At any rate, there was nothing funny about the drive home from Betty's house that night.

Had I gone to Betty's hoping to drop a hint that might
prompt her to accept the Leading Lady? I don't know. Maybe.
Perhaps I was only exploring possibilities. I'm not even sure if,
at that point, I was fully committed to the idea that Dinah
wouldn't be living with us anymore. As Patty and I drove in silence down the San Diego Freeway, I faced, for the first time,
the reality that the Leading Lady might live a life of retirement
with someone else.

Did I really have to force this change in our lives? How
could I tell our children about this momentous decision? Could

I have avoided it? Was it really necessary for me to bring
Nelson into the family? Did I actually need a new work dog,
or could I have done just fine with a cane and the people who
work for me? Was I afraid of dealing with Dinah's decline as
she grew older? Had that fear taken over now that Dinah
couldn't do her job? I'd like to think not, but in my heart of
hearts I wasn't sure.

Patty must have seen all this turmoil on my face during the
ride home, because when we were almost there she pulled the
car off the road, put her arms around me, and tried to comfort
me into believing that everything would be all right.

"Tom, you know this is the only thing you can do. Dinah
can't do the work anymore, and you want independence. It's
not just the only thing you can do, it's the *best* thing you can
do—for Dinah and for yourself."

I really needed that vindication from her. She went on to remind me of the moment I had realized Dinah could no longer
do the work and we had come to a turning point in our working relationship. I remembered it well.

Dinah and I were headed to Dallas for two days, and my pal
David Foran, who had worked with us for years, had gone a
day ahead to set up production requirements for the concert I
was going to give. Dinah and I had crisscrossed this country
with no problems—well, just a few problems—more times
than I can count. Traveling with American Airlines out of Los
Angeles International was something we had done at least once
every two weeks, and Dinah clearly knew her way around the
shining new terminal. However, from the minute Patrick, our
driver, pulled up in front of the airport, I could sense there was
a difference. There was no feeling of authority or enthusiasm
passing through the harness. I even considered asking Patrick
to accompany Dinah and me to the gate, but my chronic need
for independence precluded what probably would have been a
wise decision.

For some time, I had begun to feel changes in Dinah's mode of guiding. Where once I had felt excitement and anticipation through the harness, I now felt hesitation. Where once the harness had creaked as Dinah leaned into it eagerly, signaling a direction change, now I could hear only the sound of flopping leather as Dinah moved with uncertainty.

The truth is that Dinah was developing cataracts; it was a truth I had tried not to face. But it is rather difficult to have a blind guy *and* a blind dog in a work setting. It tends to make people nervous.

We have all been through airports, and they are hectic at best. But from the angle at which a dog sees, it is a maze of human legs moving in all directions. With the veil of cataracts beginning to cloud Dinah's vision, this great old performer had suddenly lost her confidence. Here she was, responsible for the man she loved, knowing she could not do her job as effectively as she always had, and unable to express those feelings to her master. For Dinah, it must have been a horrible moment.

As for me, I was confused, frustrated, and—I have to confess—irritated with her. Dinah was a professional. She and I had functioned for years as a team that did not even have to signal each other. My own anxiety about my blindness began to tie my stomach up in knots, and I'm sure the sensitive Dinah felt my concerns.

We had just moved through security, with a system that Dinah and I had cultivated a few years ago when the airline crisis began. When coming to the security check, I would place my bag on the moving conveyor belt and let Dinah pass through the metal detector, carrying her leash in her mouth, to the other side, where she sat and waited for me to follow.

I had called ahead and found that the airplane for Dallas was leaving out of Gate 9, a gate that could be reached after passing security and walking about 250 yards down the long corridor, taking one escalator up to a rotunda from which all the American gates fan out, going about halfway around the circle, and asking directions to the specific Gate 9 counter. The corridor leading to Gate 9 seemed more crowded than ever on this morning. Business travelers with their bags thrown across their shoulders, parents trying to keep track of running children, airline personnel with their pull carts, senior citizens trying to take their time getting to a flight, passenger service vehicles—they all made passage to our gate at best difficult and, for Dinah, now impossible.

In the past, Dinah, with a miracle blend of instinct and athletic excellence, would move me rapidly through this human wall without ever bumping into a soul. Now, in her desire to preserve my safety, this once totally assured dog became defensive and hesitant. Our pace slowed, and slowed some more. We finally made our way to the base of the escalator, a moment of safety. Dinah knew that all she had to do was stand on this moving conveyor and arrive at the top.

As in the old days, her tail thumped the side of the plastic guard rail as the escalator wound its way up to our gate level. But then we arrived at the most complicated part of our morning's journey: a circular area with no obvious clues to help Dinah make the decisions that would bring us to the departure gate.

Every blind person who has worked with a guide dog, especially with a new dog, knows the moment I am about to describe. It is when the dog becomes either frightened or confused and starts to turn in a circle, torquing the harness into odd shapes, rather than moving in a straight line. This usually brings either encouragement or correction from the master, depending on the person's mood. But when gifted, sensitive, loving Dinah, the consummate pro, began to turn in circles, my heart broke.

Time seemed to freeze as Dinah continued to rotate her body in a circle. I started to cry. I remember dropping the harness

and getting down on my knees, cradling her head in my hands.
I remember her lapping my face and whining, as if to say,
Please understand me, master. I can't live with the idea that
you might get hurt. I love you and I'm sorry.

That moment, with all it portended, was the turning point.
To be sure, we somehow pulled ourselves together and made it
out to the plane to complete our trip. But we both knew.

We returned home two days later. The time had come to
talk to Patty and the children about Dinah's retirement. The
four of us agreed that she must stop working, and were happy
she could now be a lady of leisure in the loving environment of
our home. Dinah was unaware of our discussion but it was
very much like the discussions many families have about their
aging loved ones. Although we were making life-changing decisions for her, nobody asked Dinah what she wanted. The
truth was, while Dinah could no longer perform her functions
as a Leader Dog in the way she once did, she was still not prepared to be consigned to senior citizen status without a stage
on which to perform.

My life was becoming more and more complicated with each
passing year. I knew I had to get another work animal. I hated
the idea, but there it was: I still had to make a living.

I called Dinah's former trainer, Harold Smith, Director of
Field Operations at Leader Dogs Foundation, in Rochester,
Michigan. Outside of the Sullivan family members, there is no
one more important in Dinah's life than Smitty. Considering
that she had been working for over nine years, he was not surprised by my call. I made it clear that I did not want a female
dog; there was no room in my life for another leading lady. He
promised to find me a male, and three months later he did.

So it came to pass that Nelson came to live with us. Nelson
is a black Labrador retriever who sports all the characteristics

common to the breed. Enthusiastic to the point of being off the wall, aggressively independent, he is also very loving—and he is the hardest worker, including Dinah, of all the work animals I have been exposed to. It was extraordinary to go from the elegant grace of the mature Dinah to the high energy of the young Nelson.

As I sat on the roadside in the car on the way home from Betty's that night, with Patty's arms around me, the prospect of a future with Nelson seemed bleak without Dinah's wise, mitigating presence in the background. But Patty was right. For Dinah's sake, this couldn't go on. Seeing this gallant lady in distress, I knew there was no choice. She had to go to Betty. I had to deal with my feelings. And I had to tell Blythe and Sully.

Parents tend to choose the path of least resistance when dealing with their children. In this case, I knew it would be much easier to talk to Sully about the impending change with Dinah than to talk with Blythe. Sully was away at boarding school and not due home for Easter vacation for another ten days. I could tell him on the phone.

Next morning I called Sully at school. As young people do, he cut directly to the point. Although they had not met as yet, Sully already knew that Nelson had come to live with us and was beginning to perform for me as a work animal, so his comment went to the crux of the matter.

"Will Dinah be all right?"

That was the issue. Would the Lady be okay? I couldn't answer him, but I knew that she couldn't get any worse and I told him so.

"Betty will love her, won't she, Dad?"

"Of course she will," I said.

"And we can go visit her, can't we?"

"Of course."

"Will she remember us?"

"Sure she will."

"Well, I guess we have to take good care of her, but I don't want to go with you when you take her to Betty."

"Why not?" I asked.

"Because I don't want to see Dinah cry."

I had got through my first conversation—just barely. Now I had to face my seventeen-year-old daughter, who, after me, had been closest to Dinah.

From the beginning of her life, Blythe has been incredibly hard-working and serious—much like Dinah. Things had to be done perfectly. Blythe was always afraid of saying the wrong thing or appearing less than competent, and as a result she was shy. Although she had many friends and our home was often full of little girls, Blythe's whole approach to living, even in play, was a bit formal—except when she was around Dinah.

Soon after coming to us, Dinah began dividing her nights between sleeping on the floor of our room and sleeping on Blythe's bed. I can remember often standing outside Blythe's door, listening to her speak with Dinah. She would talk about her day. She'd ask Dinah about how she was feeling. She would tell Dinah about her homework, sure that Dinah was listening to every word—as she probably was.

I remember the two of them going off to Blythe's fourth-grade classroom with all of Dinah's working equipment for Show and Tell day. How proud Blythe was of their first success together! They had gotten an "A" on their Show and Tell report.

Blythe internalizes everything, to the point of absorbing all the world's problems. How would she absorb this one? When you live with a woman/child like Blythe, you learn early to prepare your arguments as logically as possible. I began to think of what life had been like for Dinah since Nelson's arrival.

When he first came, Nelson's eagerness to play with her forced our normally passive golden girl to growl and even snap at him. I'm sure it was out of self-protection, but it was truly uncharacteristic of the Dinah we knew.

I remember the first day I planned to take Nelson to work rather than Dinah. I had put her harness and leash up on a closet shelf, because I couldn't bear to use the same equipment and also because the dogs would know the difference in the scent of their own working gear. Smitty, who had trained them both, told me not to try to prevent Dinah from seeing me take Nelson to work. Rather, he suggested that on some days I still put the harness and leash on the Leading Lady and take her for a ride in the car. We hoped she would decide that sometimes she worked and sometimes he worked. But on this first morning it didn't turn out that way.

I picked up the harness and Nelson sprang into circles of all-out enthusiasm, jumping in the air, crying, trying to get his head into the harness, grabbing at it with his mouth. He was truly excited about the work: boyish excitement, puppy excitement, a kind of spontaneity that brought me back to my early days with Dinah. And then I felt it: her head leaning on my leg, her tail smacking against my thigh. I heard the sound of her breathing as her head came up. I could feel that now there were two mouths on the harness; both dogs were pulling, both trying to get their heads inside.

I reacted the wrong way. Instead of carrying out the process the way Smitty had told me to, I pushed Nelson away with a sharp "no!" and tried to fit his harness on Dinah. It wouldn't fit and so, rather than hurt anybody's feelings, I put the equipment away and went to my appointments that day without either dog.

From that moment on, I walked a tightrope between trying to be kind to Dinah and trying to gain Nelson's confidence without offending the Leading Lady. I lost at every turn. It is not easy to develop a new friend when you are so committed to the old one. And it is not easy for an old partner to accept a new pretender.

Dinah's behavior changed radically. Where she used to have a very hearty appetite, she stopped eating. Where she once followed my every move no matter where I was, in or out of the house, she began hiding under the bed. And not even my bed or Blythe's bed. She went to Sully's empty room and stayed under his bed. She wanted no affection from anyone and would not come out to greet me when I came home from a day's work. She was unwilling to come even when I called her. I truly believe that this incredible animal was resigning herself to give up on life, to stop caring, to die. It was one of the most heart-wrenching experiences of my life.

Blythe had watched what was going on. Surely, I thought, if I reminded her of what it had been like around our house over the past few weeks, she would have to agree that I had no choice.

Our daughter's feelings, however, far outweighed my logic.

"In the first place, Dad, Dinah isn't just your dog, she's everybody's dog. She works for you, but she belongs to the family. I mean, she sleeps with me at least half the time, Mom feeds her, Sully plays ball with her, she goes on all the family trips. All the years skiing at Winter Park and summer picnics on the beach, Dinah has always been there. You can't send her to Betty.

"I don't think you need Nelson anyway. He's frantic all the

time, he's always annoying her, he's always trying to play with her instead of leaving her alone. Even Cay doesn't like him. He's never going to make it as a work dog, he's too much of a puppy. You've got David working for you. Mom can travel with you most of the time. I can even make trips with you when I'm home. You don't need a new working dog. Just keep Dinah and send Nelson back to Smitty.

"I'll tell you something, Dad, you'd better think about how *you're* going to feel when you're old. I won't find somebody to replace you. I'll always love you."

It was very hard to cope with this onslaught. But I kept hanging on to the thought that I too had some rights: the right to independence, the right to a sense of personal freedom, the right to make my own choice about my relationship with animals.

Sometimes big decisions are triggered by something minor. My final decision about Dinah was forced by something as small as a sock.

For years Dinah had played with my dirty running socks. I shouldn't say she played with them—she never hurt them—she just found them in the laundry basket and carried them around with her. She seemed to feel it was part of her job description to carry my socks around and bring them to me at odd moments of the day, and she considered this responsibility very special. So one morning when I heard the sound of growling and came upon Nelson and Dinah in a major confrontation over a sock, I knew the problem was more extensive than I had imagined.

Dinah had lost her sock to Nelson, and in that simple defeat in a doggie tug-of-war Dinah had lost her place in our home— not in *our* minds, but in hers.

It was the hardest I have ever corrected an animal. To this day I am sorry about taking out my feelings on Nelson as I ripped the sock out of his mouth and slapped him hard on the shoulder, shouting "Bad dog!" at the top of my lungs and trying as best I could to make Dinah understand that I loved her. I tried to return the sock to her; she wouldn't take it. She turned her back and crawled under Sully's bed. At that moment I knew we had to find out if the Leading Lady could lead a different life.

It was Easter Sunday, a time when families are supposed to be together. But on that Sunday it was a day when, in many ways, our family was splitting apart. Blythe and Sully had both refused to go with us to take Dinah to Betty. And the ironic thing was, when I brought out the harness and leash so that Betty would have them, Dinah thought she had been given a reprieve. Her enthusiasm shone as she pressed against me, pushing her head into the worn, familiar equipment. She worked me to our car with confidence because, even though her eyes were dimming, she knew exactly where the back car door was.

As we pulled out of the garage I heard her tail thumping against the back seat. The sound was eclipsed by the dull thump of my own aching heart.

3

BETTY

EASTER SUNDAY FINALLY ARRIVED.
No one had changed his or her mind in the cold light of
day, and *I* certainly wasn't about to chicken out. So D-Day was
here at last: Dinah Day.

During the two-week waiting period, I had told a few people
about my new adventure and received a variety of reactions. Two
of my closest friends, Rudy Behlmer and Jerry Martin, were
frankly a little worried that I was setting myself up for a hurtful
experience by taking on such an old dog. I had faced up to that
consideration myself, early on, and dealt with it. So I was able to
reassure them that I would make the most of whatever bonus
time I would have with Dinah. More on Rudy and Jerry later.

Tom and Patty had arranged to arrive in the early afternoon, so
that we would have some time to spend introducing Dinah to my

group. When Tim and Cricket's barking announced that the car had pulled up, I put them out in the back yard. T.K. the cat, though still in the house, had made herself scarce. The coast was clear.

I watched out the window as everyone got out of the car. Tom said quietly, "Door, Dinah," and, although this was her first time here, the big dog led him up the steps and into the house without pausing, her tail plume in perpetual motion. We were all playing it very cool, but emotions were running high. I am sure no one was more aware of those emotions than the sensitive Dinah herself. She simply didn't know the reason.

Almost everyone, I would guess, knows what a golden retriever looks like. Imagine, if you will, the largest golden you have ever seen, male *or* female. Enlarge that image a touch more, paint it a deep, vibrant copper, and you will see Dinah. Her figure, while no longer ingenue slim, was certainly not overly heavy. She still fit comfortably into her guide dog harness, buckled to the third hole.

Dinah led Tom to the couch, and Patty and I followed. Once Tom put the harness down and she was "at ease," Dinah and I could have our usual warm greeting. The ground rules are that you don't distract a dog while it is working; even when the dog is relaxing, *always* check with the dog's person before making any overtures. In Dinah's case, she and I had loved each other for a long time and we knew Dad didn't mind.

It dawned on me that an important member of the group was missing.

"Where's Blythe?"

Patty smiled apologetically. "She sends her love and said to tell you she was sorry, one of her friends—something at the last minute."

Tom went on to say that both kids were hurting, but they couldn't stand to see Dinah brooding her life away and realized something must be done.

"Hey, I have some good news! I called Leader Dogs to verify some dates—remember I told you Dinah was twelve? Well, they checked and she'll be eleven next month!"

Good news indeed. We had gained a whole precious year. Wait till Rudy and Jerry heard that! As I looked at Dinah, lying at Tom's feet, it was obvious that she didn't think of herself as "such an old dog," as they had put it. She and I already had a lot in common. I don't think of myself that way either.

One at a time, I let Timmy and Cricket in. Both little dogs were interested in Dinah, briefly, but then had to get on with greeting their friends Patty and Tom. Dinah's big red tail thumped the floor and her lovely face, no longer red but mime-white, smiled appreciatively.

And that was it. From that moment on it was as though these dogs had been together for a lifetime. I hadn't looked for any major problems, but I must admit this was even a little more laid back than I had expected. We all sat and visited for quite a while, Dinah in her accustomed place by Tom's side. There was no sign of her recent depression because she was back on the job. More to the point, that interloper Nelson was nowhere around.

We talked about her feeding schedule, her medical records, her normal habits—Tom's hand moving over her the whole time.

"You have a big yard, which is wonderful, but it would be great if you could take her for a walk once in a while so she'll think she's still working. And the car! She loves to ride in the car. Remember, she can go anywhere you go. She's got a lifetime permit."

We talked about the cat.

"When Dinah was in training she was taught from the beginning to ignore cats; it's a cardinal rule. But, Betty, that's when she's in harness. Jeez, I'm not sure *how* she'll react when she's loose!" Tom's warm smile was there as always, but the laugh didn't quite ring true.

Patty and I glanced at each other. Time was running out, and soon they would have to be on their way. What better moment for the boys and me to show Patty the garden?

We stayed out there a long, long time. We came back quietly, through the kitchen, leaving the boys outside, to find Tom on the floor with Dinah, his head buried in her neck. How long he had been there is between the two of them. Goodbyes are hard to say.

I went back to the kitchen and let Tim and Crickey in, this time managing to close the door with as much noise as possible.

"Oh, sorry! The wind caught it."

I put my arm around Patty and we went into the living room, to find Tom sitting on the couch where we had originally left him, his bright smile back in place.

"Well, girls, where the hell have you been? I thought you got lost out there. We really have to get back. I'll just hit the john before we get on the road." He knows my house well enough to circumvent the piano and head directly for the powder room door. As he got there he turned, still smiling. "Oh—you'd better take her harness off so she won't think she's going with us."

By now Patty wasn't in very good shape either, so I unbuckled the harness and slipped it over Dinah's head. I noticed how damp her neck was.

When Tom came back there was no lingering. We'd said it all. With one more "Be a good girl, Dinah," they headed for the car.

As they pulled away the big dog stood in the doorway with me, wagging her tail but making no effort to follow. She simply watched until the car turned the corner out of sight.

I really had no idea what to expect from my new girl. Would she sink back into her former depression? Would she be upset in a strange house, with a different family? Was she hurting as much as Tom and Patty?

"Well, Dinah, how is this, girl? Are you okay, honey?" I kept my voice bright.

For one brief moment Dinah didn't move. Suddenly she turned and bounced—yes, bounced—over to me, and we had a most enthusiastic exchange, after which she started on a meticulous inspection tour. First the house, then the garden; her whole attitude was one of positive interest. She was ready to tackle her new job.

This wonderful acceptance in no way reflected a lack of loyalty and affection for her Sullivan family. Far from it. This was simply another step in the pattern of this dog's life: Here she was at her advanced age making yet another major life change in such a seamless fashion, without sacrificing an iota of her warmth or sense of humor. That heart of hers is able to expand to include new friends without ever displacing the old.

I was to learn a lot from this girl.

Easter has always been one of my favorite times, and this particular Easter Sunday ranks high on the list. So that we would have a quiet time for settling in after Tom and Patty left, I had cleared my calendar of social obligations. This was a very important indoctrination, and there must be no distractions.

In my eagerness to make it all work I had set things up as if I were introducing a new puppy into the family, to let the dog build up her security by degrees so she wouldn't be intimidated. Well, it was becoming more obvious by the minute that I had underestimated the lady in question. Dinah Sullivan had us all figured out in the first ten minutes; she could handle anything. However, whether it was necessary or not, it was great to have our first-night family celebration with just us.

Edna was off for the weekend, so I put some chicken in the oven, along with a potato to bake, and cut up a salad. (That's about as gourmet as my kitchen skills get, but it *was* Easter, after all!) Then I fixed four pet dinners rather than the usual three, which was a nice feeling.

All my life I have talked to my pets, and I couldn't care less if I am considered weird by the uninitiated; it works. If animals are simply dealt into the conversation instead of talked down to, they may not understand the exact words, but they soon learn to pick up on some pretty subtle meanings. Their radar systems are far superior to our own.

When I put Dinah's dish down with her carefully measured portion, as per Tom's instructions, I said, "Dinah, I realize you might not feel like eating right away in a strange house and all—" Of course, she had inhaled the whole thing before I could finish the sentence.

Then I put Tim and Cricket's dishes down in their accustomed places and explained that these were off limits to big redheads. Dinah was very good that night and made no attempt to horn in on their dinners. I learned the hard way on subsequent occasions that this restraint wasn't infallible if I left the room. It took a couple of mistakes before she was totally trustworthy in that department. The two boys like to savor their food and make a prolonged production of it some nights, although they never make a move on each other's property. This connoisseur approach was a little hard for a hungry golden retriever to understand.

As far as the boys were concerned, they took Dinah completely for granted, as if she had always been there. This really shouldn't have surprised me, for, up until the last two years, both little dogs had been raised by our beloved Sooner, a black-and-tan Lab and golden retriever mix. (At least that's what we had guessed him to be when Allen and I found him on Sunset Boulevard late one night with a broken leg.) The doctor who mended him judged him to be no more than eight or nine months old. Later, when he was well enough to leave the hospital, we brought him home "just for one night, until we can find the right home for him." Funny, we never quite located that home—not in the next fifteen years.

The day we brought Timmy home, Sooner appointed himself caretaker and didn't let the puppy out of his sight. He did the same five years later when Cricket arrived (like Sooner, another unplanned foundling). No wonder the boys had no trouble with Dinah. They probably just assumed Uncle Sooner had come back as a redhead.

After the dogs had eaten, it was time to let Dinah know there was one more county to be heard from. There was a cat living here too.

Had the cat not been T.K., I might have felt real concern. However, this was the same black cat who six years ago had sat on a rock at the back of my garden for months, hunting in our ivy. I took it for granted that she must belong to one of our neighbors, and it was a long time before I finally caught on that she had no home to go to. By degrees, she had moved in closer to the house and had taken up residence on the roof of the barbecue. I hadn't fed her up to this point, as I don't think it's fair to encourage other people's pets to stray from home. But now I began putting food out for her on a ledge by the kitchen door (the hunting at our place had been good, evidently, as she was not thin!). She still wouldn't let me near her, but she found Timothy fascinating. She would watch for him, and when I let him out she'd jump down and follow him around the garden, as long as Sooner and I were out of sight. Timothy the Good-Natured thought this was just swell.

I have always adored cats, and the only reason we were without one was that, to Sooner, they were anathema. On two separate occasions I had tried to address the situation—carefully introducing two different cats. It was immediately and irrevocably clear that I was courting disaster. Sweet, gentlemanly Sooner turned instantly murderous, and both times I barely got the kitty out of his reach in time. Timmy's new friend was so wary I wasn't concerned. She would stay out of the big dog's way.

Separate from our house, attached to the barbecue, there is a large playroom. As time went on this strange cat grew secure enough to venture inside. It wasn't long before she decided it was a great place to hang out. If she heard Sooner approaching she would dematerialize and be out the door like a shadow. It all worked for quite some time: that is, until the day Sooner ambled into the room after me. I suddenly became aware that there was a black cat standing at the far end of the room; she had not done her vanishing act in time. Sooner realized the same thing one beat later and sprang into action.

It all happened so fast I could only stand frozen as Sooner made his leap at the cat. She, in turn, with every hair standing straight out and making her look twice her size, arched her back and spit at him. It was classic Halloween.

Sooner locked all four brakes and screeched to a halt. Then, with as much dignity as he could muster, he suddenly remembered an urgent appointment he had elsewhere and beat a hasty retreat.

I have never been sure whether it was because Sooner's advancing years had mellowed his hostility toward all felines or because this was one serious cat. But from that day forward, for the rest of his days, as far as Sooner was concerned that black cat did not exist. Trust me, I do not advise this kind of introduction—ours was simply a lucky accident. Too many times the same story has a sad ending.

Not long after this harrowing incident, Timmy finally lured his friend into the main house and she became officially Timmy's Kitty. Soon, T.K. chose to stay in the house permanently, and eventually the time came when she and Sooner slept on my bed together every night. Of course, as far as Sooner was concerned, it was always "What cat? I don't see any cat."

If T.K. was able to handle a street kid like Sooner, she should have no problem with our mannerly new lady. So on our first Easter evening, as I carried T.K.'s dinner upstairs to her chosen feeding place on my bathroom counter, I didn't object when Dinah followed close on my heels—very interested in yet another dish of food. Now was as good a time as any.

Teek was sitting on the edge of the counter waiting, complaining now and again with a testy meow. Rounding the corner, Dinah's take was worthy of any comedienne worth her salt. She stopped cold and there was a full fifteen-second stare-off, both cat and dog turned to stone. Then, from a standing start, T.K. made a leap that cleared Dinah's back with yards to spare and streaked down the hall. Dinah, in turn, did one of those cartoon numbers, her head whipping back and forth so fast it looked like a blur.

She made no effort to follow but turned to me with a face full of questions. Trying desperately not to laugh, I explained as well as I could. Meanwhile, the Black Maria, far from being traumatized, simply waited until we headed downstairs, then went back in, jumped up on the counter, and polished off her dinner. (It wasn't long before T.K. discovered that Dinah was such a mellow soul it was okay to use the broad red back as a trampoline on the way to the floor.)

There was one final hurdle to overcome later that first night: bedtime. Each of my three creatures of habit has staked a claim on a special place on my bed: Timmy curls up against my back, Cricket tucks into my knees, and T.K. has graduated to the crook of my arm under the covers. It isn't all that comfortable and it makes a statement about my sex life, but it *is* cozy.

I couldn't see leaving Dinah alone downstairs on her first night in an unfamiliar house, especially when she had been so people-oriented all her life. No doubt a certain cat would make other plans, but I figured we could sort that out after Dinah had been with us awhile.

I always have to read a few pages before I go to sleep each night, no matter how late it may be. If I'm tired, I may read the same page three nights in a row (I have been known to wake hours later to find the light still on, my glasses on my nose, and the book on my chest); most of the time I do better. This first night, I settled to read and Dinah came to flop on the floor beside the bed within reach of my hand. It had been a big day for her, and she was settled for the night. Tim and Crick were in their usual places. No T.K., natch.

After a few pages, I put the book down, took off my glasses, and reached for the light. As it went out, I heard a loud purr and the whole bed shook as T.K. jumped up. When cats are making a point, they can be extremely heavy-footed. I lifted the covers, so that she could plop into her usual place, her whole attitude one of patience stretched to the breaking point.

And it was as easy as that. Dinah was now a full-fledged card-carrying member of our household.

I could remember how thrilled Allen and I had been years ago when Tom first obtained this beautiful young Leader Dog.

Little did we know then. . . .

4
TOM

W HEN YOU FALL IN love, you keep trying to pinpoint the exact moment it happened. Invariably, you replay your first meeting and keep repeating "Little did we know then . . ."

All my life, I have hated auditions. From the time I tried to make it onto *The Ted Mack Amateur Hour* through my effort onstage, struggling to play the part of George in a high school production of *Our Town,* and then trying out for a summer job in the Catskills, right up to some recent frightening experiences involving TV series, auditions have been among the most difficult moments of my life. So I felt great trepidation when I had to audition for my Leading Lady.

My star had just begun to rise enough in show business so that organizations dealing with the needs of the handicapped began to think of me as someone they might use as a celebrity spokesperson. The Stroh Brewery Company of Detroit was sponsoring a ladies' professional golf tournament to be held at the Dearborn Country Club in Dearborn, Michigan; the Leader Dog Foundation for the Blind was their tournament charity. I had just begun to appear on such programs as *The Tonight Show, Mike Douglas, Merv Griffin,* and *Dinah Shore* on a regular basis, and I guess I caught the attention of the PR firm working for Stroh. At any rate, I was chosen to be the tournament celebrity player and host for the LPGA event and to promote the brewery's participation with Leader Dogs for the Blind.

Little did I know then that I would be auditioning for my Leading Lady. Little did I know we'd fall in love.

You may wonder why I say I auditioned for the Lady. I didn't realize it at the time, but the Leading Lady already knew how to do her job. I was the one who had to learn to conduct myself on life's working stage.

I had had a working dog before. One night, listening to *This Is Your Life,* I had heard José Feliciano talking about his Doberman guide dog, Sneakers, and I wanted to find out more. I eventually obtained Heidi, a beautiful German shepherd; she was a dear dog, and I loved her inordinately. She had been trained in the work, but privately, rather than at one of the accredited guide dog schools. So we weren't formally trained as a team, and though we worked together, neither of us was seasoned enough to know what skills were possible had they been properly developed. Sadly, Heidi's life ended much too early from the results of hip dysplasia. This is a congenital defect to which certain breeds are prone—among them German shepherds, St. Bernards, and golden retrievers. It occurs when the hip bone doesn't fit properly into its socket, and the condition can get progressively worse, cutting years off a dog's life. Today, responsible breeders X-ray their puppies before they sell them or eventually breed them, in an effort to identify any potential problem and stop perpetuating the condition. In Heidi's

case it got so bad we finally had to put her down at six years
of age.

After that heartache, I decided it was unnecessary for me to
become involved with another working guide animal. I never
again wanted the pain of losing another work partner. I was
very good with a cane. I had musicians and others working for
me who could help me whenever I needed it. I thought of myself as more independent without the attachment to the harness.

But I guess I'm a product of the industry I work in because,
influenced by the Stroh publicity people, who believed that
their event would be enhanced if Tom Sullivan, golf tournament host, received a brand-new dog from the Leader Dog
School in Rochester, Michigan, I agreed at least to talk with the
director of training, Harold Smith.

Smitty changed my life. He has been training dogs for
twenty-eight years, four of those years for the Air Force. He
not only loves the dogs he works with, he respects them. He
may even know more about dogs than he knows about people.
His ability to read a dog, to understand its every nuance, to
have almost direct language communication is one of the most
remarkable phenomena I have ever observed. Our friendship
was instant. We liked so many of the same things: sports, good
food, endless conversation usually shared over a few cold beers.
And our children: Smitty has two also, Tracy and Todd, and I
think it's fair to say we all sort of grew up together.

At any rate I met Harold Smith a few months before the golf
tournament, on a trip to Detroit to do publicity for the upcom-
ing event. I was making records for the ABC Recording
Company at the time and performing in concert for thousands
of screaming kids, traveling on the road and living the rock and
roll lifestyle. When he asked me what I was looking for in a
dog, I tried to make it impossible for him to fill my order.

I needed a dog that was totally adaptable, I told him—an

animal that wasn't frightened by loud noises, in this case my music; a dog who was comfortable in all forms of transportation, ranging from planes and buses to the backs of trucks loaded with equipment, to limos if I had acquired a good gig; a dog that could handle strange hotels, varied time schedules, inconsistent diet, lack of sleep, constant petting and attention from strangers, a master who stayed up too late and wasn't always ready to take his canine friend for a walk at six in the morning—and on and on and on. After making this strong case against ever having a Leader Dog companion, I wound up by saying, "Smitty, you'll have to prove to me that I need a dog."

Smitty had listened carefully. "Tom, I guess you don't really *want* a dog, but I'll tell you something: you sure do need one. Your life is so hectic. But for you to experience true independence, you need something that can think and feel and be consistent in its love. Something a lot warmer than the end of a white cane. You need a dog. But I won't kid you; the animal you're looking for is almost impossible to find. And I also won't lie to you. Just because you're a celebrity and the school wants me to find you an animal because they think it would be good publicity, I am not about to turn any dog I love over to you unless you truly want it and unless the match is perfect. So unless I find you the animal that is ideal, and unless you prove to me that you two can be a great team, I'm not about to put my reputation on the line and just provide you with a pet."

From that moment on I respected Smitty, even when we disagreed, and our friendship will last for life. I went home to Patty and the kids, sure that I had demanded too much and that those demands, coupled with Smitty's integrity, would make it impossible for Leader Dogs to find me a working animal. Thank God I was wrong.

·   ·   ·

As the months went by, I purposely did not contact Harold Smith. In fact, I avoided communicating with Leader Dogs altogether.

The day before I was to leave for Detroit to host the Stroh golf tournament, the phone rang. Smitty's voice came down the line.

"Hey, Sullivan, I've found the best animal this school has ever produced. The question is, are you going to be loving enough, talented enough, and good enough to deserve her?"

I remember thinking, That's pretty confrontational. Who the hell does he think he is? I got a little sarcastic myself. "I can handle it. When can I meet this Superdog?"

"How about if I bring her to see you at the hotel in a couple of days? You're staying at the Hyatt Regency, right?"

"Yes."

"Then I'll see you in a couple of days with Dinah. She's a golden retriever, she's smart, she's beautiful, she's loving, and she's tough. Just the combination you're looking for."

What the hell was he talking about? I wasn't looking for anything, but I love challenges, and the idea that this guy thought he had a dog I couldn't handle interested me a lot.

We were going to the golf tournament as a family. For seven-year-old Blythe and five-year-old Sully, it was one of their first trips on an airplane and one of their first chances to stay in a major hotel. They were ecstatic, and the idea that they were going to meet a special dog too made the trip to Detroit a lot easier for them—and for Patty and me.

So it was July 14, 1977, when a young golden named Dinah came to visit her new family. When the knock came on the hotel room door, the kids rushed over to let Dinah and Smitty in. The first thing I remember as the door opened was Dinah's tail, rhythmically banging the doorframe, and then I heard the sound of her leash and collar as she was immediately embraced by two excited children. When I asked Sully about it the other day he said, "Dad, I can remember that Dinah had a big tongue, and when I put my arms around her neck we rolled on the floor and she licked me, and licked me, and licked me."

I remember that too. The sound of Sully's laughter made me realize that if this dog didn't work out as a guide dog, I would still probably have to try and make a deal with the school to own her.

Blythe's memory was much more feminine. "Dad, I remember how beautiful she looked. Her head was up, and she had that special glitter in her eyes that's still there today, that says, 'I love life, I love people, I love my work.' I remember her tail was straight out, whipping from side to side as she walked, and there was a sense of incredible noble pride, without any feeling of coming across as—oh, too pompous."

When the tumult quieted down Smitty said, "I'd like you to meet Dinah."

I placed my hands on that soft coat and immediately loved the feel of her. As I put my hands on her neck, she reached up with her mouth and gathered up the leash that had been dangling from her collar, as if to say, "Let's go to work." She still does that today.

Smitty laughed. "I guess she's ready to do her thing, Tom. Are you?"

I was a little taken aback. I figured there would be some preliminaries or something before we found out if Dinah could work for me. That Smitty sure was confident.

"Okay," I said. I picked up her leash and placed her harness in my left hand. The instant I picked up that harness, Dinah responded. Her body tensed. Her tail and rear end began to shake with anticipation. She wanted me to tell her what to do. But— what to do?

Smitty said, "Let's take her downstairs."

I said, "How do you want me to do that?"

"Just give her a command, Tom. You know how to do it. You've had dogs before."

"Okay, Dinah, find the door."

She moved instantly to the hotel door, putting her nose right on the knob. That's an instinct you can't teach an animal. Most of them will just arrive at the door area, but it was important for Dinah to complete the task with precision and enthusiasm.

"The elevator is around the circle to the right," Smitty said. "Just keep following Dinah. Give her a positive suggestion to find the elevator door, and she'll do it."

I opened the room door and said, "Dinah, right. Find the elevator, girl."

There was not one second's hesitation. Dinah turned right and walked the forty or so yards to the bank of glass elevators without a pause or a backward step. She put her nose right on the down button. Now, in all fairness, she certainly didn't know it was the down button; she had just been taught to find the button in an elevator. But for me it was impressive. Heidi would not have done that. Few dogs would be so exact. I began to understand why Smitty felt Dinah was so special.

The Hyatt Hotel in Dearborn, Michigan, is one of the most prodigious architectural structures in America. It is built on an atrium system: all rooms on all floors face out over a towering central lobby. The thirty-seven floors feature a glass-enclosed elevator looking out over the city skyline: enough to frighten children, their parents, and most certainly a fourteen-month-old golden retriever Leader Dog named Dinah. But when we got in the glass elevator, Smitty explained that he had been training Dinah here for the last month, and that was why she wasn't afraid to look out over space.

We arrived in the crowded lobby, and with my command to "Go outside," Dinah weaved her way through the foot traffic

and took me out the swinging doors. She stopped, question-
ing, as her paws touched the different surface of the hotel
parking structure.

Smitty said, "Tell her to find my car."

"Are you kidding, Smitty? She can't find the car."

"Of course she can, Tom. Her smell is all over it."

"Dinah, find the car."

Her head went high in the air. Her nostrils flared, and I felt
her sureness and purpose as she moved through the hundreds of
cars parked in the Hyatt garage and placed her nose on the
driver's side of Smitty's TransAm. Wow! I couldn't believe it. I
couldn't believe any animal was able to do this wondrous
thing. For me it was truly remarkable. For Dinah, I found out
as the years went by, it was just another day on the job.

Over the next five days, Smitty, Dinah, and I tried all
kinds of tests, from going in and out of stores on make-believe
shopping trips, to cruising busy streets as well as those in quiet
suburban neighborhoods, to walking routes that Smitty designed to try and confuse Dinah and me, to entering and
leaving all kinds of office buildings, to going to the airport and
testing Dinah on the jetways. We tried to cover all the circumstances she would confront when she entered the real world as
my Leading Lady. But nothing we could do could anticipate
the life that Dinah was going to live. The simple truth was that
no other guide dog in history would ever be thrown into such
a topsy-turvy, always changing world as the one ahead of
Dinah, with a naive master who assumed that she was immediately ready to take on full responsibility for the job.

In all the manuals written about the relationship between a
guide dog and a master, the emphasis is placed on easing the
dog into the work process. It is suggested that the initial days
of work be spent in your own familiar surroundings, on easy

neighborhood walks of never more than fifteen minutes, and with the dog feeling successful in every way at the completion of each work session.

There is a phrase in the circus where trapeze artists, flying above the center ring, talk of working without a net. Although Smitty accompanied us on those first days, and although we might say he represented Dinah's safety net, he was uncompromising in his commitment to force Dinah and me to work out all our own situations. He might step in with a suggestion or a device for me from time to time, but never—I repeat, never—with direct aid, and I am sure the looks he got from people as we stumbled around in the middle of hotel lobbies and airport terminal corridors were hostile and hard to take.

At the end of five days I knew I would become inseparable from this beautiful golden girl. I was infatuated by now, certainly. Perhaps not yet truly in love.

The Leader School decided it would be a terrific idea if, during the golf tournament, Dinah was presented to me in Detroit on the television show *Kelly & Company*, a popular daytime hit. They pulled out all the bells and whistles. I played the piano and sang and then Smitty brought out the fourteen-month-old golden girl, with a bow around her neck and the audience wildly applauding, to make the presentation in a mock ceremony.

Years later, on a book tour, Betty made a guest appearance on *Kelly & Company*. Because her book was on animals used in therapy, the co-hosts—two delightful people, John Kelly and Marilyn Turner—casually mentioned how moved they had been a few seasons back when Tom Sullivan had received his Leader Dog on their show. They were surprised to learn that we were friends and that Betty knew Dinah as well. No one

could have guessed then that someday Betty would know
Dinah much, much better.

When the golf tourney was over, Smitty and I agreed that
Dinah needed another month or so of polishing and fine-tuning
to help her adapt to what promised to be, euphemistically, an
unstructured future. Even though Smitty was sure this dog
could do the job for me, he wasn't sure that I, with my aggressive Irish temperament, was the right person to spend a work
life with this refined golden girl.

"Time will tell," he kept saying. "We'll see if you measure
up, Sullivan."

I left Dinah in Detroit for her postgraduate work, and
Smitty began to customize. He worked to accommodate all the
special things that her life with me would entail. As well as
drilling constantly in airports through all the pedestrians, PA
systems, and people movers, he also taught her to recognize
what "piano" meant, so she would be able to guide me to what
was at that time my tool of the trade.

Smitty had told me how he had chosen Dinah for me in the
first place. "She was by no means the only dog on my string—
I work nine dogs a day—but she caught my attention. No matter what I asked of her, she kept accepting more. It was like,
'I've got that; what else?' This dog was so eager to please she'd
stay with it until she got what you wanted!"

He told me that in order for things to be easy later on, it
took some doing in the beginning. The glass elevator, for example. Smitty said the first time Dinah got into that glass box
and it began to move—straight up, yet—Dinah cowered and
dropped to the floor, all four legs straight out. Talking, petting,
and general reassurance did the trick, and it wasn't long before

she took that challenge in stride. Escalators too were a little confusing but, making a game of it, Smitty overcame another hurdle. I understand some guide dog schools don't encourage using escalators because there could be a potential hazard, but moving stairs soon became old hat to this girl, whose feet were big enough not to get caught.

I returned to California, looking forward to our reunion. What I didn't know was that, although an audition can go perfectly, rehearsals, opening nights, and performances can be far more complicated, filled with mistakes and frustration. The audition had gone well. The jury was still out on how Dinah and I would do on the big stage.

5

BETTY

E HAD AGREED ON Easter Sunday, when Tom and Patty had brought Dinah to me, that it would be a good idea to give the Lady a little period of adjustment before we spoke again.

Tom stood it for almost a week, but then he couldn't wait any longer for reviews on his girl's performance.

Needless to say, they were glowing. How good it was to be able to tell him that not only was Dinah active, she was extremely busy. Already she had sorted out the pool man and the gardeners from the postman and the UPS driver. Dinah and Edna were the best of friends, and she had taken full charge of Timothy and Cricket.

As for her reaction to T.K., once again it was a case of "What cat? I don't see any cat!"

It couldn't have been a better report.

"One of the dearest things she does is the slipper thing in the morning."

There was a short beat of silence at Tom's end of the line before he said, "What slipper thing?"

It wasn't like Tom to be slow to catch on.

"You know, the way she hands you your slippers every morning when the alarm goes off. That may be old stuff to you, but it knocks me out!"

"She never handed me my slippers in my life! What the hell are you talking about?"

Well, once again, I had not given Dinah enough credit.

The first couple of mornings she had been with me, she had seen how all the bodies had come to life when the alarm rang at six-forty-five. After a little community yawning and stretching, I would invariably sit up and slip my feet into my slippers (guess that's why they're called that), and then everybody would follow me downstairs to be let out into the yard for their morning's morning. By the third day, when the alarm rang, I hit the snooze button as usual, for that delicious extra ten minutes, my eyes still closed. I could feel the bed gently shaking, and I opened my eyes to find a blue slipper in my face, held by an extremely cheerful red dog. She was leaning her chest against the bed, so with every wag of her tail, the whole bed moved.

Of course I thanked her, took the slipper, and said, "How 'bout the other one?"

As if it were standard operating procedure, she picked up the remaining slipper—and while she didn't exactly *give* it to me, she let me take it from her. A twinkle in her eye indicated this would also make a great come-and-get-me game, if I was so inclined. From that day to this, our morning routine has remained the same. The blue slippers are pretty tired by now and I'm sure a new pair wouldn't change anything, but I'm sticking with these until they fall apart. (Later: they finally did, and it didn't.)

When I told Tom the story, he flipped. He couldn't get over the fact that even after nine years, she could still surprise him. I also think his Irish feelings may have been a tad hurt that she hadn't done the same for him.

As the days grew into weeks, Dinah built up her own routines. Her new role seemed to fit her like a glove, and there was not a trace of her previous depression.

When I'd run errands or go to the market, she often tagged along for the ride. Tom was right; she loved the car—but bless her, there were very few things she *didn't* love. Possibly only Nelson and lettuce.

I remembered what Tom had said about taking her for walks so she would feel she was still on the job. This was a pleasant assignment, and on weekends, when I wasn't working, we'd often go out, either very early in the morning, around sunup, or just before dark in the evening. I tried to pick times when we were less likely to meet other people, since Betty White walking a guide dog in harness took a little explaining. Wouldn't the tabloids have a ball with that one?

Taking a walk with the working Dinah was a fascinating experience. I tried very hard to let her do the leading, which, when one is sighted, is easier said than done. Your reflexes tend to take over and send all the wrong messages down through the harness.

Using every bit of willpower I could muster, I would force myself to relax as totally as possible. Dinah was all business—a different dog from the one I knew at home. I could feel her pull on the harness, not lunging like an amateur dog tugging at his lead but strong and steady, with just enough tension to let me feel a change in direction. As we approached an obstacle in our path or over our heads, Dinah would firmly guide me around it with room to spare.

At first I tried closing my eyes, but this only confused the issue. Working with a guide dog is not something you pick up on the first try.

Neither is blindness.

As was to be expected, Edna had fallen in love from the word go and soon got used to fixing dinner around a golden planted in the middle of the kitchen floor. Edna's only reservation was that Dinah's gentle nature and sweet friendliness would keep her from being much of a watchdog.

Privately, I was tempted to agree, but what did it matter? That certainly wasn't the reason she was with us. We already had a built-in early warning system in Timmy and Cricket. It's good to be made aware if anyone is approaching, and the little guys are great at that job. True, they get a little overcommitted to their work. They let you know if someone is jogging past the house or if a truck drives up the hill on the next street or, on occasion, if a leaf happens to fall the wrong way. A sharp "no!" is the off switch.

From the beginning, it was apparent that Dinah evaluated all of this, and if the situation warranted her attention, she would add her bass notes to the staccato—but only if someone turned into our driveway. Don't ask me how she knew this, lying in "her" spot on the cool floor between the throw rugs in the living room. She couldn't possibly see from there, and if she was judging by what she heard, it was filtered through the barking of two small dogs. She *had* to be reading what they were communicating.

It wasn't long before the question of Dinah's protective capabilities was answered. We had been having some sprinkler work done at the back of the garden, and the plumbers had stopped by very early one morning to do some adjusting. Unaware of this, I had let the dogs out as usual and started to fix my coffee. I was suddenly conscious of Dinah barking at a distance in a voice I had never heard before, and I went to investigate.

There she was, standing in the middle of the back lawn, four feet planted, tail straight out, and perfectly still (I didn't even know her tail could stop wagging). As I approached, the barking changed to a low, throaty growl, but she never took her eyes off the two men.

Fortunately, Richard and Tom had done work for us for years, and both men were dog lovers. The moment she heard me greet them, Dinah relaxed into her own sweet self and came up to be introduced. She remained slightly less enthusiastic than usual, however. Why hadn't they come through the house in the normal fashion? What were they *doing* there?

Where were Timmy and Cricket all this time? For one thing they knew the plumbers, but also, that part of the yard was out of their jurisdiction. An invisible line runs clear across our property, separating the lawn and garden behind the house from the pool and back garden beyond. Tim and Crick are not allowed to cross this imaginary barrier for any reason. *IT IS THE LAW!* I established the line years ago when Timmy was brought home as a new puppy. That first day, the pool looked like blue ground to him, and he walked right into it—not once but twice. Also, our property goes down a hill with thick ivy and trees. While it is strongly fenced, I swear that coyotes can fly, and I had seen them in the yard several times. One tiny black poodle would be just a tasty tidbit. No matter how carefully anyone might intend to watch, I wasn't about to gamble on one unguarded moment. Tim had to have some rules of his own to follow.

It only took part of two days before he got the idea. I would wait until Timmy put one foot over this imaginary line; then I would say a very sharp "no!" I'd slap the ground on the wrong side of the line, repeating "*no! no! no!*" Of course, if he stopped before he crossed over, I would be extravagant in my praise. I must have looked and sounded like a congenital idiot.

I did this all across the property, from fence to fence, so he couldn't outsmart me by going around. There was also another invisible barrier across the front door, which is the only access to the street. This had been established long ago to keep four-footed friends from dashing out if the door was open. Believe me, nutty as all this sounds, it works.

I had had every intention of establishing the same "imagi-no line" when Cricket joined us, but it was never necessary. Timmy must have taken care of that lesson immediately, because from the beginning there might as well have been a wall there, as far as both little dogs were concerned. This was especially surprising, in light of how young Cricket was when he joined us—not quite six weeks, according to the vet.

Crick and I found each other quite by accident on the final stop of a fourteen-city book tour. The book, *Betty White's Pet Love,* was about animals used in therapy. Beyond the dogs that work with the blind, there are Hearing Ear dogs, such programs as Canine Companions for Independence, and Handi-Dogs for the handicapped, pet-assisted child psychotherapy, prison programs, therapeutic horseback riding, and a host of dog and cat programs for the elderly, from visitation to permanent residence, as well as the hospice cats for terminal cases. Because of the breadth of the subject matter, every talk show I did in every city would include dogs and cats from the local shelters. That's a dangerous game for someone with my susceptibility, but somehow I managed to give them all back, even a certain white Pekinese in Houston . . . a close call.

I finally made it to Oakland, the very last city before heading home, where we were to inaugurate a pet therapy program at the Oakland Children's Hospital. The Oakland SPCA had sent over three puppies and a bunny for the occasion, to spend a little time with the children. There was a white puppy and a brown puppy, and then there was this little cream-colored job about the size of my wallet. He had been brought to the shelter the day before by a man who found him on the street. As appealing as he was, he was a natural for the launch of this program.

When the young patients were brought in they had a wonderful time being able to touch these animals, and I was gratified to see how gently the children handled them.

One little girl in a wheelchair with a portable IV was enchanted by the tiny cream puppy, who eventually fell asleep in her lap. The child's IV ran out, but she didn't want the nurse to change it, for fear she would "wake the baby."

I was booked on a flight back to Los Angeles early that afternoon, and after fourteen cities I couldn't wait. The bunny and the puppies, after a job well done, were on their way back to the SPCA, hopefully for adoption. Although he was way too young to be on his own yet, the little cream one was so adorable that he would have no trouble finding takers. But he was still so fragile, I worried about the damage eager, rough young hands could do.

I boarded my plane, but the anticipation of getting home was clouded by the thought of that tiny creature. I couldn't get him out of my mind. Let's face it, I'd fallen hard!

As soon as I arrived home I put my bags down and headed for the phone. I called the Oakland SPCA and told them not to do anything about that puppy—he was mine!—and two days later I flew up to claim him. Not until then did I discover that no live animals are allowed on any flight out of Oakland. Now I had to get someone to drive me across the bridge to San Francisco to catch a United flight back home.

The course of true love is never without its problems. By now this was getting to be one of the more expensive little free dogs, but it was all worth it. He proved to be truly my magic cricket, and he helped me through a very low time in my life. He could always make my beloved mom laugh through that whole last bad year.

He was such a baby when he came home, it was no wonder I

was amazed to find that he was aware of the invisible barrier from the beginning. He and Tim would be bouncing at my heels as long as we were in their part of the garden. But let me cross the boundary line to go pick flowers out back, I'd turn to find this pair of black and white bookends sitting side by side waiting for my return to their territory.

With Dinah I never established such a barrier. The running room out back would do her good, and she is big enough to take excellent care of herself. It was astounding to watch them go tearing out, Dinah heading straight down the hill but the two small fry peeling off and turning back when they had reached their line. Talk about the honor system!

Neglecting to make Dinah aware of the front-door line was a mistake that could have been costly. One day I came home from work, received the usual royal welcome from everybody, and headed upstairs to change my clothes. Evidently I had been so carried away with my greetings I hadn't slipped the dead bolt, and the front door hadn't quite caught. In a few minutes when I came back downstairs, the little ones at my heels, of course, I found the door standing wide open—and no Dinah.

I ran outside in time to see a flash of copper disappearing down the other side of the street. In my panic I did exactly the wrong thing: I screamed "*Dinah!*" As accustomed as she was to instant response, Dinah didn't miss a step. She wheeled and came bounding back up the middle of the street, straight into my arms.

Cars speed up and down our street all the time, and it was no credit to me that she made it safely. How stupid can you get, calling a dog across a road without looking or getting on that side of the road yourself? To this day, when I think of the trouble my bad reflexes could have caused, I still turn cold. Curiosity had led Dinah out the door, but she hadn't done

anything wrong according to the information she had. I had
been the dumb one. Twice.

After about three weeks, since she had adjusted so smoothly,
we all decided it might be time for Dinah to see her family again.
Tom called Smitty just to check and make sure he didn't think it
might upset her. Smitty agreed with us that this girl could handle
anything required of her and that it would be a fine idea.

Patty invited us for one of her heavenly dinners, and as luck
would have it Nelson was away that night. It hadn't been planned
that way, but he was spending two nights at the veterinarian's.
For some reason, eating a matched pair of Tom's socks hadn't
agreed with him. (When he came through fine, Tom said, "He
can think of it as a learning experience!")

Patty and Tom live about an hour's drive from my house, and
as usual Dinah stretched out on the back seat of the car, watching
for a while but then sinking into a comfortable doze. When I
made the turn off the highway her head came up, and when I
turned into her old street she sat up with interest.

The whole family (sans Nelson) was there at the door, and the
greeting was delightfully abandoned on everyone's part. Both
Tom and I were happy to notice there was no nervous anxiety or
underlying hysteria. Dinah greeted each one and rolled over on
her back, not caring that she was a dignified, mature lady. She
also did her bouncing number, where both front feet leave the
floor in a series of short jumps that will rattle the dishes in a
cupboard. I call it her "camel dance."

Tom didn't do a camel dance, but his joy in the Lady made my
throat ache. He stood back quietly, letting Blythe and Sully have
their full time, and then Patty. Dinah worked her way through
them, through Cay and Season, and then proceeded to absolutely
eat Tom up, wrapping herself around him again and again.

When we eventually settled into the playroom, she flopped down in her accustomed place by Tom's chair, lying under his hand, smiling, enjoying the conversation, much of which was about her. Tiny Season, the Maltese, spent the entire evening on my lap, telling me how unappreciated a small dog was in a house of such big animals. I didn't buy a word of it, not with Blythe around, but sympathized appropriately.

We had so much to catch up on. The time seemed to fly until we were called in to dinner (you can tell how much help *I* was— but I had to hold Season!).

The table was so pretty and the food of course delicious. And with this group of loving big talkers there was never a lull. Suddenly Tom interrupted.

"Excuse me, but look where Dinah is! Is anybody aware of what that means?"

Dinah was lying behind my chair, close enough so that she would know if I moved to get up. When I tried to say she had just settled there by mistake, Tom shook me off.

"Dinah doesn't make mistakes like that, and you know it. She's never lain there in nine years! Have you any idea how happy that makes me? Hey, she likes her new job!"

Later, when it was time to start for home, Dinah said her warm good nights, then gathered up her leash in her mouth and headed for the car.

All the way home I marveled at Tom's sensitivity. He was the one who had noticed Dinah behind *my* chair at dinner. It also said something about his nature that, thinking of Dinah's well-being, he celebrated the fact rather than give in to an understandable twinge of jealousy. Class all the way.

It wasn't until I talked to Tom the next day that I realized I might have been guilty of a touch of wishful thinking.

Tom called early, before I had had a chance to phone my thanks for a delightful evening. He was chuckling.

"Boy, as you drove away last night you must have heard that collective sigh from the Sullivan family. It was hard to believe what we had just witnessed. Dinah had come to our home—her former home—as a perfect guest." I didn't hear the chuckle anymore. "Dinah! A guest!

"After you left, Sully said, 'I think Dinah loves us, Dad,' and Blythe said, 'Of course she loves us, but I don't know if she misses us!' "

Before I could respond, Tom continued.

"Patty and I think it's just great that she's so happy. How about that greeting! And when she moved over to your chair so easily, as if to say, I understand my new job!"

"How did it make you feel, Tom?"

"I'm just ecstatic that she's doing as well as she is!"

"Tom, old buddy—this is me. How did it make you feel?"

"I found it very difficult to accept."

It was very quiet for a moment, before Tom went on.

"It's a lot like being a parent. We want our children to grow, and yet we want them always to need us. I've always needed Dinah, and now I want her to need me." The laugh reappeared as he admitted, "I fought with some very conflicting emotions last night, ranging from childish jealousy to pride in how well balanced Dinah was. She's a creature who truly understands herself. I guess I wound up somewhere in the middle—relieved at how well this experiment has turned out."

For my part, I was glad we were able to talk openly about this, instead of letting it fester in the dark somewhere.

Later in the conversation Tom said, "Last night when Sully was going to bed he asked me, 'Dad, will Dinah keep remembering us?' I tried to explain to him that of course she'll remember us, but maybe a little less and less."

In this case I am happy to report my good friend was totally wrong. We have all continued to get together every few weeks, but now when it's my turn we stay home for dinner, so Dinah can be part of the party. Over the last four years Dinah has become more and more comfortable in her new environment, and I think seeing her here has helped both Blythe and Sully feel better about the whole situation.

Dinah gets very excited each time they come, treating all the Sullivans as if they are family members coming home for Christmas. It is a greeting unlike that for her other friends. It is special—saved for her family alone.

Dinah's list of "other friends" is a long one that continues to grow.

For years the Sullivans and the Luddens have used the same limousine service to go to and from the airport. We travel a lot on business, Tom even more than I, so the drivers have become like family. They often relay messages back and forth between our two houses.

I used to love hearing the reports on Tom and his wonderful guide, Dinah. Each driver would describe how, the minute he drove up in front of the Sullivan house, Dinah would come running out and jump in the car to wait for Tom.

Sometimes Patty would be going with them, and (according to Dale St. John, owner of Town and Country Limo, who *has* been known to exaggerate) when the Lady would see Patty's luggage, the golden ears would droop. Oh, damn! Is *she* coming? That would mean Dinah wouldn't have Tom all to herself. Patty and Dinah love each other dearly, but sometimes it is a little tough for a star to share the spotlight.

So when her limo driver friends found their pal at my house, it came as a surprise. Now they vie for my call—not to see who drives Betty, but who gets to say hello to Dinah!

·   ·   ·

Another friend of mine, Wayne Ferguson, fell under Dinah's spell immediately. Wayne lives in New Jersey and is a fellow trustee on the board of Morris Animal Foundation (an animal health organization), as well as vice president of their Canine Division. Wayne owns one of the largest mail order pet supply businesses in the country, and to a still playful if slightly mature golden retriever, Wayne and his Cherrybrook Company are choice friends to have.

Wayne has designated my four animals as his West Coast research team. Every promising new toy that comes on the market is sent out here for evaluation. Timmy couldn't care less, as he likes people, not toys; T.K.'s enthusiasm depends on how much catnip is involved (I hate to use the word *junkie*); so Dinah and Cricket are the consumer advocates, and they give a great review to almost everything that comes along.

Dinah's particular favorite is a six-foot-long fuzzy pink snake. She'll do a five-minute routine, tangling herself up and then trailing it behind her like a fading movie star's old mink. After all the years of hard work, her enthusiasm at this age is remarkable, even compared to the much younger Cricket. But then, Crick has the attention span of a moth and gives up early on.

I have already mentioned my friends Jerry Martin and Rudy Behlmer and their concerns about my taking on a dog of such advanced years. I knew once they had met her they would feel better about the situation, and there was no way they weren't going to love her. What I hadn't counted on was that they would both become her slaves.

Jerry Martin is my commercial agent, as well as a very dear friend. While always there for support, he doesn't just tell me what I want to hear; he is not above pointing it out when I screw up. Probably thinking this was one of those times, Jerry had to meet Dinah as soon as possible. He loves dogs, and as his apartment situation rules out having one of his own, he has enjoyed being Uncle Jer to Timmy and Cricket.

So the day after Dinah moved in, Jerry came over to check her out. Predictably, he was captivated on sight, and I don't think he's been off my den floor since.

By now you may have gathered that this Superdog is without a flaw. True, but for one exception, which is no fault of hers: she sheds. Copiously. Even though I brush mountains of golden hair out of her almost daily, there seems to be no end to the supply. When Jerry is picking me up to go out for the evening I shut Dinah in the den until we leave, just for the sake of his clothes, but I have to promise both of them some time together when we get home.

It is no different on the nights when we have to attend those all too frequent black-tie charity functions. When we get home at the end of the evening I go upstairs to "slip into something more comfortable" and come down to find Jerry, Dinah, and the tux on the den floor. At least he takes his jacket off! That poor tux goes home each time looking like a dog suit. I've often wondered what interesting pictures are conjured up in the mind of Jerry's dry cleaner.

Rudy Behlmer, if anything, was worse.

Rudy and his lady, Stacey Endres, are both very fond of dogs and were planning on getting one of their own as soon as they settled down. Now, I have known Rudy for over thirty-five years, and in all that time, as far as he was concerned, there has been just one breed of Real Dog: The Beagle. The only decision left to be made when it came time to acquire a dog was whether to get one or two beagles. Stacey wasn't quite as rigid, but if Rudy's heart was that set, a beagle it would be.

Enter Dinah.

If truth be known, the big redhead does play to the house

sometimes, and when she has a receptive audience she abuses the privilege. The night they all met she outdid even her usually charming self, bringing her toys (Cricket's, in reality) to show, rolling on her back, playing coy—you name it, she did it. When the time came for our next evening together I was invited to their house with, "Can Dinah come over to dinner?" I'm sure I was only included to provide transportation.

Chalk up four more conquests for the Lady. In the case of Rudy and Stacey, however, it didn't stop there. They must have one of their own: not a beagle, not just a golden retriever, but a mature golden retriever with Dinah's working background.

Rudy knew that, in lieu of giving business gifts each Christmas, I sponsor a dog with Guide Dogs for the Blind, located in San Rafael (up in northern California) by underwriting all its expenses. He asked if I could steer them in the right direction toward finding one of these special animals.

Easier said than done. I called both Guide Dogs for the Blind and International Guiding Eyes, another school, located in Sylmar, California, and was told by both that a retiree was virtually out of the question. In most cases the old dog stays with its master and readily adjusts to the change in lifestyle when a new dog comes in.

International Guiding Eyes said we might have a chance to get one of the dogs that flunked out. Guide Dogs for the Blind put it more diplomatically, saying that sometimes it was possible to acquire a dog that was in "career change." Both organizations explained that there was a long waiting list.

Hooked beyond the point of no return, Rudy and Stacey immediately went on the list, prepared to wait for as long as it would take.

Well, Dinah, here was another fine mess you got us into!

Finally, the long-awaited call came from San Rafael. There was indeed a fine young female golden retriever who might be just the right dog for them. The only thing that had kept her from passing her final exams was that she had tested as being a little skittish at loud noises.

And so it came to pass that Elsa, at a year and a half, moved in to live with Rudy and Stacey and become the light of their lives.

Exit The Beagle. There is nothing more zealous than a convert.

Smaller and slighter than Dinah (ingenues always are), Elsa's color is the same deep shade of copper. The two girls get along beautifully when they visit back and forth, and both Tim and Cricket have no problem with the idea that two girls are better than one. It is interesting to note that there is no sign of depression or competition when the big dogs are together. But then, no one is after the same job, as had been the case with Nelson.

Once in a very great while, Rudy and Stacey mention a beagle puppy for sometime in the distant future, but now it's "So Elsa can raise it." In the meantime, Elsa has an established routine. Every morning, rain or shine, work day or weekend, Stacey and Elsa work for twenty minutes, so that her early training will be reinforced. Elsa's, not Stacey's.

Watching the young Elsa, so eager to please, so bright, already so committed to her family, I tried to picture Dinah at that same age. Was my sophisticated Lady ever that naive? It was hard to imagine.

6

TOM

WHEN DINAH'S POSTGRADUATE WORK was finished, Smitty brought her out to us in California. After spending three days on my refresher course, Smitty returned to Detroit and Dinah and I were on our own.

When the Leading Lady and I first began to work together, I was amazed to find myself with an acute case of stage fright.

I have always refused to think that people in any profession suffer from what can be called true stage fright if they believe in themselves and their skills. However, if you place a human being in a circumstance in which he or she must perform in something that is not necessarily within the personal comfort zone, it can be an entirely different story.

Let me give you an example. In 1976, when I walked out onto the playing field of the Orange Bowl in Miami to sing the national anthem at the Bicentennial Super Bowl, I was not afraid. Yes, my knees did shake. Yes, there was a sense of excitement that went from my stomach all the way up through my body to the top of my head. But it was not a feeling of fear, it was a feeling of anticipation. I knew my job. I knew how to sing. I knew that with a little help from a higher power and good concentration, I could give a memorable performance. The same thing applies to astronauts being shot into space. They are excited, but doctors report that their pulse rates cannot be construed as anything but normal.

Yet in the beginning with Dinah there were two things that spelled danger. First, as I said, I had stage fright—the real thing—and I'm sure I conveyed that fear from my hand through the harness right to the brain, heart, and soul of the Leading Lady; and second, in my desire to fulfill the great potential that Smitty had said the Lady and I could achieve together, I was much too demanding.

We'd only been together a few days, this young golden girl and I, and she was barely settled in when I decided it was time for us to have a major adventure.

I thought we would take a normal kind of stroll from my house to the beach, jog two miles along a bike path to the Redondo Beach pier, stop, have a cold drink, jog two miles back, and then simply walk home. It seemed easy enough, especially since Smitty had worked on jogging with Dinah. And today, after years of experience with the Lady, it would be. But just a few days after she had arrived, it was a task comparable to Sir Edmund Hillary climbing Everest or a new jogger deciding to run the New York Marathon.

Chalk it up to youthful enthusiasm, or youthful arrogance, but I put the Lady under a stress that was totally unfair and could have ruined a lesser animal. I also chose to take this journey on a weekend, when the bike path leading to the pier area would be crowded with bikers, runners, and strollers. It was an unbelievably naive approach to early work with a new dog.

Anyway, off we went, noontime on a Saturday. It was a

picture-perfect California day. From our house Patty could
look out over the whole California vista, from Malibu to Cata-
lina and back again. God had clearly smiled. Dressed in only
shorts and running shoes, with a couple of dollars tucked in my
sock, I headed off. My enthusiasm was so unbridled that not
even Patty chose to suggest I might be biting off more than I
could handle, and my kids thought it was a great idea. I remember saying, "I'll be back in about two hours." That would
have been two o'clock. At eight-thirty that night, people were
still looking for me.

From our house to the entrance to the Redondo Beach bike
path it is a mile and a quarter through a residential neighborhood. This immediately spelled trouble. You see, when the
Lady learned her work at school, Smitty taught her patterns:
follow the sidewalk to a curb, stop, wait for the command to
go forward, then cross to the nearest and easiest access to the
sidewalk on the other side. Recognize that traffic might be
pulling out from other street crossings and watch for it. Guiding around objects consisted mostly of things that Dinah had
seen in training: telephone poles, fire hydrants, overhanging
trees, that kind of stuff. What the Lady found on this first venture into freedom were things she had never dealt with before.

In our neighborhood, Saturday means garbage collection day.
The sidewalk was strewn with cans and bags of all types. Cars
were suddenly pulling out of driveways. People's trees were
very rarely cut back, and the path was constantly overhung
with objects that Dinah was forced to watch for, from the perspective of her height, and try to gauge whether or not I might
clear them. Sometimes there would be no sidewalk at all, and
Dinah was obliged to pick the safe shoulder with traffic whiz-
zing within inches of her new master. Also, Saturday is a very
busy day and people were not cautious, to say the least. Horns
beeped, voices complained, and sometimes a good Samaritan
would leap from his car trying to be helpful, grabbing us and

turning the Lady and me in a wrong direction. People had never seen Dinah before; this was a new phenomenon, and my neighbors weren't familiar with the idea that Sullivan now had a new lady to take care of him. But at least until we got to the beach, my confidence remained high. It was a beautiful day, and I was on an adventure with my new Leading Lady.

It's interesting—no, it's sad—to recognize that I had no idea of what was going on in Dinah's mind. I can imagine what she was thinking: If this is what my life is going to be, please send me back to Smitty.

I was also much too aggressive in my correction of her. Whenever something went amiss in this initial walk, instead of considering whether I was responsible for it, I blamed Dinah and constantly gave her harsh vocal corrections, along with snaps of the leash, as I had been told to do when I thought the Lady was wrong. Looking back on it, my friend did not make one mistake. I made thirty-seven.

The hardest thing in the life of a blind person is not achieving independence but coming to terms with the idea that one can never actually *be* independent. When I want to play golf, someone has to line up the shots. If I want to ski, someone has to guide me down the mountain. And up to this point, when I wanted to take a run I had to hope that one of my friends was interested in doing the same thing at exactly the same time I was, or change my schedule to accommodate someone else. And through it all I felt compelled to be the ebullient, nice person. The person who makes conversation. The person who is always a positive force. Because I was the one asking for help. Can you understand how much the freedom I expected to achieve with the Leading Lady meant? "Free at last. Thank God almighty, I'm free at last!"

That's how I felt. But as with the civil rights movement, freedom has a price, and I soon found out what that price was.

Before giving her to me permanently, Smitty worked for three months teaching Dinah to jog. But all his training had been under controlled conditions on the paths surrounding the school or on quiet residential streets. Remember, too, Smitty could see where he was going. He could help Dinah. Also, though Smitty would not like to admit it, he's not in the greatest shape; he certainly doesn't jog or run as much as I do. (I know when Smitty reads these pages, I'll hear about *that* comment!)

At any rate, Dinah and I got to the bike path and began running, with my unbridled enthusiasm pushing the Lady to her limits. The bike traffic on the path is one-way, staying to the right, and we ran with the traffic, not against it. Consequently, on our two miles to the pier, the run was easy. All the bike traffic was coming over Dinah's left shoulder, as I hugged the right side of the path.

We got to the pier with no major incident. I was unbelievably excited. I am sure some intelligent psychologist might determine that I was more crazed than just delighted. You see, I was experiencing the first moment of true independence in my whole life.

I stopped for some juice at a small cafe on the edge of the pier and sat there listening to Mexican music as the sun beat down on my back. And I did something else that was unconscionable. I forgot about water for the Leading Lady!

It was sheer thoughtlessness; in my enthusiasm, I assumed that dogs were in much better shape than people and could easily outrun them. Actually, dogs have only one source to reduce heat in their bodies, and that is through their tongues. Here I had the Lady running on hot summer cement, the heat pouring through her paws, wearing the pads down, carrying that luxurious fur coat—while I asked her to run and run and run. Brother! I had been running for ten years, I was in shape; would I ask my mother to go out and take a four-mile run without preparation? Would I ask anyone to do that? Absolutely not. But I demanded it of the Lady. I not only demanded it, I expected her to love it. I was sure that she would continue to guide me efficiently, even though she was tiring. It is hard for me to comprehend that I was that naive. Thank you, Dinah, for surviving the cruelty of my ignorance.

Anyway, after satisfying my own lavish thirst, we turned and started back. Now I was really excited. A cool breeze was beginning to blow. It was now late afternoon; the waves crashed in on the California coast. I realized I had spent more time than I thought, but I was completely involved in the sense of my own freedom and the joy of that experience.

On my beach a blind person can count fourteen different kinds of waves that can be heard as you jog along. On some mornings when I've run on the sand there are eleven different textures to touch; more different kinds of birds than you can count dot the skies, and their cries delight me. There is a potpourri of sensory awareness that is limitless: the smell of the ocean, the scent of mock orange mixing with restaurants selling their delicious wares, suntan oil and diesel fuel. All these smells, tastes, touches, and sounds paint my sensory panorama, and on this day I loved it all. On this day I wasn't paying attention. On this day I got hurt.

On the way back, Dinah and I had to run against oncoming bicycle traffic. Although required to stay to the right, when the path gets crowded bikes have to find space where it's available. My pace had quickened now. I was driving the Lady. My own athletic ego had my feet pounding the pavement, reaching for that Zen runners speak of. An oncoming biker was doing exactly the same thing. Head down, buried in his helmet, leaning over his handlebars in a racer's position, he was exerting maximum effort. Two fated human beings on a collision course.

I know Dinah saw him. I know she jerked the harness, pushing hard right. I know these things happened, but I don't remember the impact. It's funny about crashes; when they really hurt you don't feel them. It's as if you are saved that pain—that is, until you come to again.

I was probably out for only a minute. When I came around I was surrounded by runners and bikers, concerned about whether I was all right. But none of them was as close to me as the Lady herself. She had burrowed under my shoulders and neck, my head rested across her back, and at the same time she was trying to turn her neck to lick my face. Sounds came from her as close to the expression of human concern as an animal can muster: "Are you all right, master? Are you all right, master?" she seemed to be saying. "I tried—I'm sorry, I'm really sorry!"

Having been a competitive athlete all my life, I know to stay down while assessing injury. Voices were asking that most unanswerable question, "Are you all right? Are you all right?"

"I don't know," I said. "I need to try and sit up."

The pain shot through my body. My ribs felt as though they had been caved in, but I was sure I hadn't broken anything. Having done a lot of wrestling in college, a violent sport, I knew that. But while nothing was broken, I felt like Muhammad Ali had hit me with a fifteen-round body barrage.

I'm forty-two years old now. If this happened to me today, I would accept help. But at thirty, with a substantial self-image based on machismo, I said, "I'm fine. I'm fine. We'll be all right." I was probably even rude in forcing people to leave us alone.

The Lady never stopped licking, never stopped pressing her body against mine. Through the haze of pain I became aware of her intense concern. There are moments in one's life when you realize profound truths. This was one such moment for me. I realized that the Lady had done everything right. I had been the person who messed up; she had done all she could while I wasn't paying attention to the signals. I put my arms around her neck and said, "Sorry, girl, I guess I wasn't watching where we were going. Let's go home."

That seems like a simple thing. Let's go home. It turned out to be a nightmare. We hobbled our way to the end of the bike path. There was no way to mess up this part of the journey; it was a straight line. I could have done it even without the Lady. Thinking back now, I realize I may have been concussed, because when we started up the path from the beach I had no idea where I was.

It is impossible for a guiding animal to work under those circumstances. The master has to know where he wants to go. It was especially important in this instance, since Dinah had never been to the beach before. We arrived at the top of the path, above the beach, and turned completely in the wrong direction. It was about five in the afternoon by this time. I smelled charcoal as people were starting their summer night barbecues, I could hear kids playing stickball in the street, parents were probably getting ready to go out for a Saturday evening, and the Lady and I were walking, walking, walking. Assistance was available, but old macho Tom wasn't willing to ask for help. Unbelievably, even in my hurt state, I was unwilling to lapse back into that world of dependence. I was going to pound on to victory. In my own ego-centered way I kept saying things that Smitty had told me to say. "Come on, Dinah, let's go home. Find the sidewalk. Find the street. That's the girl. You can do it." And the Lady did. She kept giving and giving and giving. She had no idea where she was taking me, but I was encouraging her to work, and she would go on until she dropped dead from exhaustion.

Finally, my body ached to the point of collapse. When a blind guy begins to see colored lights and stars in front of his eyes, it's time to stop. My stop came in the middle of somebody's front lawn. It seemed as good a place as any to collapse, as reasonable a place as any to die.

I actually thought I might die; maybe somebody should come out of his house and shoot me. Not the Lady, of course, just this old dying blind guy. "Yup, let's put him out of his misery. He wasn't a bad guy, but he won't be of any use to himself or anybody else in his condition."

I must have fallen into some kind of dreamless sleep, because the next thing I remember was the Leading Lady. This time she wasn't licking. She had my arm in her mouth and she was pulling. Not too gently, either. It hurt. I did something unpardonable. I swiped at her with my other hand and hit her—pretty hard, too. She yelped, jumped back, and grabbed my arm again. As far as she was concerned, her master was going to get up. We weren't going to stay on this front lawn forever. So there we were. I was back on my feet and we were moving. Some kids were on the street playing.

"Hey, are you all right, mister? What's that dog do?"

I answered woodenly, "She's a seeing-eye dog, can't you understand that? She guides me."

"Well, where are you going, mister?"

"Home," I said. "Except I guess I don't know where that is."

What a profound thought. Had anyone ever before had such a profound thought? Finally, my defenses broke down.

"Hey, kid," I said. "Are your parents around?"

"Sure, mister. Just a minute."

Safety. Ed Jackson came out of his house, took one look at me and the Lady, and knew we'd had enough.

"Hi, I'm Ed Jackson. Are you lost?"

"I guess I am," I replied. "Any shot that you might give me a ride home? The address is 2201 Via Rosa. It's the house right across from St. Francis Church."

"Boy," he said, "you're a long way away. Four or five miles, anyway."

"I know," I said. "My dog knows it, and my feet know it."

And how about Patty and the kids during all this time? They had been driving all over the neighborhood for the past three hours, asking anybody if they had seen a golden retriever dragging a blind guy around. My legend must have spread. They'd heard all about me but hadn't quite caught up. As we came around the corner entering Via Rosa, my street at last, Patty was just pulling into the driveway to call the police.

To say the least, she was frantic. She seemed to try to grab us both at the same time. Oops! There go the lights and stars again. It sure hurt when she hugged me, but it was worth every bit of the pain to be loved, to be cared for.

To be loved, to be cared for. That's what I had learned this day about the Leading Lady. She loved me, and she was doing everything possible to care for me. It was now up to me to determine how to love her and how to care for her, and how to have a life that would remain fulfilling and valuable to both of us. I knew what had to be accomplished—but how in hell did you get there? I needed help.

When a man is drowning he grabs for the nearest life preserver. In my case that lifesaving cushion was Smitty. I called him in Detroit and told him our story.

He listened quietly. "I hope we haven't ruined that wonderful animal, Sullivan."

"What do you mean, Smitty, how could we have ruined Dinah?"

"Because I gave in to pressure to let you have her too early, and because you were too aggressive in using her. Sometimes these animals never recover. If that's true in this case, neither one of us will ever be able to forgive ourselves. I'll be out there in two days. Don't work her at all, do you hear me? I mean it. Don't even go near the harness until we see what her situation is. Sometimes these dogs are traumatized to the point where they will never work again. We'll see." He hung up abruptly.

I was shocked. Dinah seemed the same: she came when I called her, wagged her tail and rolled over on her back to have her stomach rubbed for affection, was eating normally, and all in all seemed no worse for the harrowing experience. Maybe I wouldn't take his advice. Maybe I'd just find out.

I decided to take her for a simple car ride with Patty, something that would only force her to work from our house out to the driveway and into the back seat of the car.

I went to the closet to pick up her harness and leash. Normally when this happened Dinah was alive with anticipation and joy. She would leap to my side, thrusting her head into the harness and trying to bite it at the same time with happiness. But when I picked up the harness on this particular day, Dinah ran away. She literally ran away—out the back door and into the yard. When I followed her, telling her she was a good girl, she made it a point to stay well out of reach. She obviously had been traumatized and wanted no part of guide work.

I was truly shaken and horrified. What had I done to this dog? It was a very humbling experience for someone who needed to be humbled.

. . .

Smitty arrived two days later.

It was as if Dinah were transformed. She had only been with us about a month, but she had worked with Smitty for many months previously and was completely bonded to him. From the minute he entered our house and greetings were exchanged, Dinah was Smitty's dog and wanted nothing to do with me. I had heard through the school about this kind of thing, but when it happens to you it's absolutely devastating. The ego is a delicate part of the human condition. And whom did I resent for this intrusion? Not Dinah, Smitty! Smitty, the expert; Smitty, the competent; Smitty, the man who could do no wrong with dogs. I was angry at Smitty! And more so when I found out that Dinah was delighted to work for him.

When Smitty took out the harness and leash, there was no hesitation, no pause or fear or trepidation. Dinah only wanted to work, and that is what they did for the first two days. *They* worked. I never got near her. Smitty asked Patty and me to show him all the places I might even consider wanting to go with the Leading Lady, from the beach where we tried our run, to the stores I like to shop in, to Hennessey's Irish Pub.

The tension in our house was palpable. Because Smitty was staying with us, the time when he wasn't working Dinah meant that we needed to entertain him, something I didn't feel like doing. But Smitty is a very bright fellow; he kept the dialogue up. He talked to Sully about motorcycles and bicycle racing. He was charmed by Patty's new decorations in our house and her gourmet skills in the kitchen. He went with Blythe to her riding lessons and talked with her about working with animals. And all this time he kept exposing Dinah to more and more stimulation.

And who was on the outside looking in? Me. I was fuming by the third day, when he told me it was time for me to begin to work with Dinah. And so, instead of approaching the job with enthusiasm, I came at it as if I was trying to win a major athletic competition. I wanted to do everything exactly: put the harness on with precision, bark the commands with authority and definition, apply too much praise, be too aggressive with my hand signals and body language—all of these behaviors, I'm sure, winding Dinah up inside to the point of wanting to run away again. But if so, she didn't let on. She had regained her enthusiasm for the work.

Smitty, however, was aware of my attitude.

He tried to caution me—softly in the beginning. "Remember, Tom. A dog is like a car. It will take you anywhere *if* you know where you want to go. Be sensitive."

But finally he snapped.

"This is an exceptional dog, Sullivan! I don't think you appreciate what you have!"

We were at a street corner, and when I didn't stop properly, we really got into it.

Smitty yelled at me. "Do as I instruct! This dog doesn't know you're a celebrity, she couldn't care less. You're all 'I, me, my, you owe me! I want!' In order to *want* you have to *give*!"

I was hacked. I started away, still without giving Dinah a sufficient signal—and fell over her up the curb.

All I could say was, "Jeez, now I know what you mean." But perhaps I still didn't.

It took four days of hard work before Smitty agreed that it was time for Dinah and me to try a solo.

I was to go down three streets, turn right, cross one block, turn right, and return the three blocks to the starting area: a very easy square, something done at the beginning of guide dog training for all blind people. Smitty explained that he would stay out of Dinah's vision, and so, for the first time since our traumatic run, Dinah and I would be alone as far as Dinah was concerned.

I was like the neophyte actor debuting on the stage, commanding and praising Dinah in a voice much too loud, trying to move ahead down the street with too much pace and too much English on the harness. English means aggressive use of your left hand holding the harness, to try to get the dog to do things—all of these together being like a rider kicking his horse too often to get the animal into a canter.

Dinah took this process quite well, but I'm sure her concentration was rattled and not as good as it usually was. Because as we moved down the second block I was struck in the head by the limb of an overhanging tree. Now, overhangs are the kinds of things good working dogs are taught to look for; however, don't forget that from the dog's point of view, an overhang is easy to miss.

I overreacted. Maybe it was the emotions I had built up over the last few days, but I stopped and angrily corrected Dinah, snapping her leash hard and telling her "Bad dog!" in a voice that was usually heard only by Patty in the worst of our domestic arguments.

Smitty appeared out of nowhere and without any preamble said, "I'll take my dog, Sullivan. You follow me."

"What the hell are you talking about?" I said. "She's not your dog, she belongs to me."

"Oh, no, she doesn't. Read the small print in your contract. The school holds the right to reclaim an animal if it is being misused or mistreated. As far as I'm concerned, this beautiful girl is being misused."

Grudgingly, I put my hand on Smitty's arm and followed him back to the car, which he had parked in the middle of our route so he could observe us from a distance. We got in in silence and I thought we were headed home but instead, as the car came to a stop, I heard the familiar strains of the Irish song "Wild Colonial Boy" drifting from Hennessey's tavern.

"Get out, Sullivan," Smitty said. "I'm buying."

And so in we went for a few pints of Guinness, a shot of courage, and the beginnings of a friendship.

After the second Guinness, drunk in silence, Smitty said, "Why do you think I'm so tough on you, Tom?"

"Because you're a jerk," I said. "Because you're a guy who can deal with dogs but not with people."

Smitty laughed softly. "Maybe you're right, but I don't think so. I think it's because I believe that maybe you two can be the best Leader Dog team I've ever produced, and I'm going to be horribly disappointed if it doesn't work out. You both have all the skills it takes, if you'll soften and become more realistic about what Dinah can and can't do.

"Look, you have to remember first that she can't actually read your mind. Sometimes she can interpret what you feel and sometimes she can outguess you, but she is not the Amazing Kreskin. She is a dog, the purest of all God's creatures. Absolute honesty, absolute love, absolute commitment—that's your Dinah. And do you know what, Tom? If you don't have that agenda understood, you shouldn't have her.

"I feel so guilty that I allowed the school to pressure me into giving you this incredible dog before either one of you was ready. I told you you had to go slowly at first, and not ask her to do something that even a seasoned animal would have trouble coping with. After working her myself for a couple of days, I'm sure she is going to be all right. That is, if we can just settle you down a little and build the mutual confidence you need in each other."

"What have I been doing wrong?" I said.

"Everything, Tom. From the way you speak to the way you handle the harness. The harness is your attachment to Dinah, but you have to let her make the decisions, not plow ahead like a bull in a china shop. When I watch you work, you're much too far forward. You don't allow time for the harness to register the dog's feelings in your hand and arm. Give Dinah time to make the choices. Don't press through. So often, when you trip or bang into something, you blame Dinah, when in effect you have outworked the dog. That overhanging tree today—if you'd seen her eyes—she looked up and saw it, she hesitated, she gave you harness language; you just weren't sensitive enough to understand it."

"Wait a minute. Goddammit, Smitty, if you knew this when you sent us into the field in the beginning, why did you let us go?"

Smitty sighed. "Because my bosses told me to, Tom. Because you're a celebrity and they wanted the national attention that you receive on television.

"Remember when you were given Dinah on *Kelly & Company*? You wouldn't believe what Dinah was going through backstage that day. She heard you singing and playing the piano, there were lights everywhere, cameras rolling, a tile floor to cope with that made her slip—she was panicked. It was terrible. Remember, usually when dogs are presented it's in the school, where they've lived for months, where they are comfortable and secure. We were also forced to accelerate her training with you so I could get her to California in time for your fall concert schedule. We only worked together a few days—we should have had a month! Everything was too fast. Everything was too political. I should have had the integrity to slow things down. You're not the only one at fault, Tom. So am I."

We started to talk about other things. Smitty had been born and raised in Michigan, and right out of high school he had gone into the Air Force, where he discovered his love for training canines. This service background, along with the fact that he had seen Leader Dogs at work throughout his childhood, brought him back to Rochester, Michigan, and the Leader Dog School.

He talked about his feeling for the work. "You know, another reason I'm so tough on you is that so often I'm forced to send these dogs into the field with people who should never have them. I mean people who treat them as pets, not as work dogs. One of the great problems in our profession is that the dogs are always qualified, while the people are only qualified maybe a third of the time. Too many dogs go to too many blind people who don't use them appropriately. That concept has to change.

"Then there are my problems with the people who get the dogs. I've had everything happen to me, from having to cope with guys who want to beat my head in because they think I'm being unfair to them during the training, or because I have to go to their homes and take their dogs away, to women who fall hopelessly in love with their trainer. It's like the stories you read about women who fall in love with their therapists. I face blind people at their most vulnerable and exciting moment, the acquisition of a canine friend. It opens up all kinds of emotions, not all of them healthy. I was married, you know."

"I do know that, Smitty. You've told me about your children, Tracy and Todd."

"Yeah. I guess the principal reason I got divorced was because I was also married to the work. It's kind of tough to do both." He went on. "I love these dogs. You really learn to understand them, watching their eyes, seeing their expressions, reading their concerns. I've never met a bad dog, only frightened ones, and they're not responsible for that."

As I listened and drank my Guinness I began to care about this man. I understood that his intensity was all about devotion to the work. How could I criticize that? And in turn I began to tell him about my hopes as a songwriter, my dreams of being an actor. We talked about realities—about my need for independence, about my childhood struggles for acceptance among my peers and why those struggles tended to make me too aggressive.

And he, just as frankly, told me I would never be totally independent. At best, I would become interdependent. That is a concept I have learned about over the years.

By the time we left Hennessey's Irish Pub we were mutually attached, to each other and to Dinah. As she sort of led both of us home, we decided to leave Smitty's car right where it was. Discretionary drunks, the best kind.

When we had left Patty earlier, she had been aware of the tensions that had been building between Smitty and me over the past days. So her surprise was understandable when these two good buddies arrived home at last with their dog. It must have been like the classic scene from *The Quiet Man,* when John Wayne and Victor McLaglen arrive back at Wayne's home and demand dinner from Maureen O'Hara following their legendary fight. We were drained of anger and delighted with each other, and we solemnly swore to go back to work the next morning.

Frankly, we took the next day off and went to the beach, nursing our hangovers in the Pacific. But when we did return to work, it was with a new purpose and new patience. I know Dinah must have felt these things, because there was never another backward step, and over the subsequent days the work began to be not only fun but second nature.

Curbs were found easily. My harness skills grew more accurate. My overall approach to command became softer and much more relaxed. Dinah's enthusiasm was back full force, whether I was working her or Smitty was.

We did everything. From the normal curbs where Dinah would come up to the edge, placing me in line to cross the street, to what are called "flush curbs." These are the street crossings in which there is no actual step-off, just a break in the pavement that challenges the dog to put the master right on the edge, often without the master understanding that the "curb" is even there.

We worked in and out of stores, particularly grocery stores

with narrow aisles, forcing the Lady to change her gait and forcing me sometimes to slide my body in behind hers, rather than being perfectly parallel. We worked hard on finding an empty chair in a crowded room. Dinah is one of the few dogs to actually go up to a chair and place either her paw or her nose on the seat. Most dogs just get to the chair in a general way.

On we went: elevators, escalators, up and down steps; in and out of all kinds of building doors, including rapid-fire revolvers; country traveling—that is to say, working on roads with no sidewalks, using the shoulder as our guide path.

There were the traffic checks, where we would cross the street and then Smitty would race around the corner in his car, forcing Dinah to stop immediately to avoid being hit. Cat checks—making sure that Dinah was not cat sensitive. Other-dog checks—finding out if Dinah would play or fight with dogs she encountered in the work. Overhangs; we worked them and worked them and worked them, until both Dinah *and* master were sensitive to the fact that they might be there.

The difference between the work we put in over the next two weeks and the training I would have received at the school was that Smitty focused only on Dinah and me, not on a class where the number of dogs and the number of students are approximately ten to a trainer. The other thing that happened was the growth of understanding between Smitty and me. Just as Dinah was beginning to understand who I was, I was beginning to understand who Smitty was: a man of great commitment, infinite patience, and huge levels of awareness. For me he was no longer just a man who trained dogs, he was my friend.

We were back in Hennessey's again, at the end of a very hot and extended day. Everybody was tired. The beer tasted good, both to Smitty and to me, and there was a sip for Dinah.

He said, "I'll be leaving, Tom. I've done everything I can do for the best team I ever created."

I put my glass down abruptly. "You mean that, Smitty? Are we really getting there?"

"Tom, I'm confident that when you two 'season' over the next year, nobody who has ever had a dog will do a better job. Just stay soft, stay loving. Dinah will do the rest."

I knew that would be easy from now on, because I did love her and I knew I could work her effectively.

"When is your next trip planned?" Smitty asked.

"Oh, in a couple of days. Chicago."

"Okay. Why don't I plan to go on it with you on my way home? Let's just see how this team does on the road."

Dinah's and my first airplane flight together was to take me to Chicago, where I was to perform at a banquet for the Better Boys Foundation. This organization is supported by the National Football League Players Association and the caring citizens of Chicago, all to benefit needy young boys throughout the metropolitan Chicago area.

I had naively decided that Dinah and I would tackle this job absolutely without help. That is to say, from the time Patty dropped Smitty, Dinah, and me at the Los Angeles airport, Dinah and I really would achieve getting to the Drake Hotel in Chicago alone. Smitty would be along, but staying at a distance as a silent observer.

This trip was made before the need for airport security became so compelling, and clearly before LAX had become a significantly modern metropolitan airport. There was no modern parking garage, no attractive new terminal with soft music playing as you make your way along moving sidewalks to waiting aircraft. There were no helpful clubs, like the United Red Carpet or American's Admiral's Club, where a passenger could go for special assistance. It was simply: get out of your car, push open a swinging door, hear the din of an echoing, cavernous airport lobby, and try to wind your way along forever tunnels, searching for your gate and your airplane.

We also faced another phenomenon that was not one of the Lady's favorites: tile floors. It seems like such a small thing. But to a Leader Dog, who must exert tension on the harness, tile floors are akin to skating on ice.

As Smitty explained later, when a dog gets nervous and attempts to dig its nails into a surface, it begins to slip even more. So picture this scene: an overconfident blind man, expecting absolutely perfect work from an anxious new golden girl, steps onto a slippery tile surface expecting to feel the authoritative pull of a harness and instead feels the nervous retriever trying harder and harder to exert guiding pressure, while sliding as if she were trying to do triple spins in the Olympics with Dorothy Hamill.

As time went by, Dinah did adapt and so did I, over the course of many airports. We eventually learned that, on tile, the secret is to move slower across the surface, with slightly less forward chest-pull stress on the harness and with a tangible effort on both our parts not to start and stop. It is a lot like learning to drive on the icy roads of New England in the middle of a cold January. But this first time, how did the master handle the situation? In typical klutzy fashion, I encouraged Dinah to work harder.

"Let's go, girl. You can do it. Come on, girl. It's all right. Hop up!"

"Hop up" is the standard command that encourages any guide dog to try even harder. So there we were, slipping and sliding our way around the Los Angeles airport.

In my desire to try to do everything on my own, I had instructed Smitty not to even give me gate information. I was going to ask a passerby to please read the television monitor announcing out of what gate Dinah and I would be flying.

Imagine my shock when the first three people I asked for

help were from South Korea. Consequently, their response was either to ignore me or continue to say, "Sorry, I'm so sorry, no English, sorry."

My next victim was a lovely old lady who was having her own struggle searching for the airplane that would take her to Des Moines, Iowa, to visit her grandchildren. Then came the New York businessman who, in clipped Manhattanese, informed me that my gate was 34 and that I should go "that way." An interesting phrase to a blind person—"that way." He may even have pointed in the appropriate direction, who knows. But now Dinah and I at least understood that it was gate 34.

We finally slipped and slid our way to the gate, coming to a skittering stop in front of a surprised ticket agent, who obviously had never had to board a blind person with a guide dog before. The first problem arose when she tried to explain to me why I needed to rent a kennel and have Dinah fly in the belly of the aircraft. At that time many airplanes were not pressurized, and many animals died in the bellies of those aircraft. In the mid-1970s airline personnel knew very little about working dogs and even less about blind people.

Once we surmounted that hurdle, with my anger level becoming higher and higher, she then insisted that Dinah and I be placed in the very last row of the coach section of the airplane, along with a mother with two children, both under five years of age.

Once on board, these children believed that Dinah had been sent from heaven specifically to entertain them. In the course of those next few hours they pawed, mauled, pulled, and stepped on the golden girl.

Stoic Smitty allowed it all to happen. His view was, "It goes with the territory."

These days, as I fly with Nelson, crisscrossing the United

States as a first class passenger, I realize how much easier his
life is with his master.

As the children mauled the Leading Lady and their mother
said things to me like "You don't mind if little Johnnie pats her,
do you?" Dinah became more and more nervous. Remember,
she had only been up in one airplane before, the one that had
brought her and Smitty to California, and although they had
gone to the airport often to practice while planes took off over-
head, there is quite a difference when suddenly those jet
engines turn over and a dog, lying on a perfectly level floor, is
lifted into the air and then thrown back against the seat. Also,
we were sitting in the back of the aircraft, where the noise is
much louder. The fact is, the girl panicked. She shook so hard
it felt like her ribs might be breaking. She drooled and whimpered and, in the course of our takeoff, tried desperately to
climb up into my lap.

Smitty had chosen to sit four or five rows ahead of us on the
airplane so Dinah could not see him. One of the hardest things
in the work is to break the dog away from her trainer and turn
her over to her new master. The full completion of this turn-
over generally takes more than a year, and here I was asking
Dinah to function under unbelievable pressure with Smitty taking away her support system. And then there was little
Johnnie's sister, who wanted to give Dinah all kinds of treats,
ranging from a Nestle's Crunch bar to anything off her break-
fast tray.

The next stage of our trip went quite well. We arrived in
Chicago and, coming off the plane, found some very nice people to ask how to get to baggage claim and taxis. My
confidence was beginning to come back—that is, until we arrived at the Drake Hotel and were greeted by a front desk
reservationist who did not think the hotel allowed pets. By this
time I had lost it. I not only had a few choice words for this an-

noying man, I demanded to see his manager and, I hope, got him fired.

Dinah's next challenge was my music rehearsal. Smitty and I had not been able to prepare Dinah for this, and as the twenty-four musicians wound it up to play the first number, supported by Fender Guitar amplifiers and a very aggressive drummer, the golden girl freaked. From her place next to me at the piano on stage, she leaped from the platform and raced the length of the banquet hall to Smitty and protection.

I don't think Dinah ever really came to like my music; at best she came to tolerate it. That is also probably the view of a number of critics. But I persisted, and my records paid for a lot of dog food. Our first day ended with Dinah needing to have an extra long walk to relieve her system and my tension.

It was time for Smitty to head back to Rochester and regular training. In parting he made it clear that he felt very good about Dinah and her friend and their future together.

I wished him good luck with his next case and told him I hoped it would be less complicated than this one had been.

"Gotta be, Tom, gotta be." I could hear his grin. "But it may not be as much fun, either." So the training wheels were off and Dinah and I were officially a team, heading down the road on our own.

ACT TWO

7

BETTY

*T*HE BETTER I GOT to know Dinah, especially watching her outthink most other dogs I've known, the more curious I was about the "how" of her. How did she learn all the things that had become second nature to her? How did she manage to bridge the communication gap that exists between her species and ours so successfully? What training process enables her and others like her to become the incredible working animals they are, without sacrificing any of the great natural dog within?

The idea of using a dog to lead the blind is far from new. A Germanic king is said to have been the first to do so, somewhere back around 100 B.C., and artists have been depicting dogs with the blind since the first painting of a dog assisting the blind, uncovered in Pompeii on the wall of a house that had been buried in lava in A.D. 79! It wasn't until World War I, in Germany, however, that these dogs really came into their own to assist young men who had been blinded in combat.

Word of their accomplishments spread, and they were subsequently introduced into the United States. Today, there are some ten schools of varying sizes in this country, training dogs to work with the blind. While they are not affiliated in any way, their goals and procedures are similar. Representatives of these schools come together on a yearly basis to exchange ideas and progress reports, always seeking to standardize and improve.

Of these schools, the original was The Seeing Eye. They were the first to introduce the concept in this country, back in the twenties, and they continue their magnificent work and tradition today in the beautiful rolling countryside near Morristown, New Jersey.

I had a lovely visit at Seeing Eye headquarters and was taken through their fine school and kennels and surrounding property. I did the same at International Guiding Eyes, another good facility, in Sylmar, near Los Angeles. Ironically, however, I had never made an actual on-site visit to Guide Dogs for the Blind in San Rafael, up in northern California, in spite of the fact that I had been in contact with them by letter and by phone for many Christmases in arranging dog sponsorships.

San Rafael, California, is some hundred and fifty miles north of Carmel, and it was always too easy to peel off at Carmel to spend that precious time, promising myself I would make my long-intended visit to Guide Dogs "next trip."

But after receiving such wonderful cooperation in obtaining Elsa for Rudy and Stacey, I decided it was high time to remedy that situation. On my next trip north, I called from Carmel and spoke with Jennifer Conroy, Development Director at Guide Dogs, who had been so instrumental in finding Elsa. I asked if it would be convenient if I drove up sometime in the next few days for that long-promised visit. Her response was an immediate "yes," and her warm enthusiasm made me feel as if she were welcoming a friend, rather than handling an obligation to a visiting fireman.

"How about tomorrow?" she said. "It's about a three-hour drive." And she proceeded to give me wonderfully clear directions.

Next day, I left early and in spite of morning traffic near San Francisco, including detours around bridge repair after the earthquake, I was just about on schedule when I pulled into the beautiful complex that comprises Guide Dogs for the Blind.

Jennifer had invited me to arrive in time to join the "students" and their new dogs for lunch. The dining room was airy and spacious with a number of round tables, each seating six people. Under each table, in various postures of total relaxation, lay six assorted fledgling guide dogs: German shepherds, Labrador retrievers, both yellow and black, and golden retrievers.

Some of the students enjoying lunch that day were first-timers. Others were back for their second, even a third dog, and it was fascinating to hear anecdotes from the different perspectives.

After lunch, I was taken on an in-depth tour of the entire plant, and what a special place it is.

We began by making the rounds of all the offices to meet the staff, and each and every office we entered had at least one dog, usually two, permanently ensconced with bed, toys, and an abundance of personal attention. Some were career change dogs, owned by the personnel, and they came along to work every day; others were breeder dogs or retired Guide Dogs who were just hanging out.

It was nice to meet another telephone friend in person: Bette Wilcox, who had also been helpful in Elsa's transition to her new home with Rudy and Stacey.

"I was so happy that Elsa found such a loving family," Bette said. "I fell so in love with her that—well, I got carried away. Meet Jubilee."

Sure enough, Jubilee, another "career changer," was very much like Elsa, a slim young golden, perhaps a shade more blond. Natural.

Dinah's outreach again. Because of Dinah, Elsa found a new family; then Elsa, in turn, led to Jubilee's new life with Bette Wilcox.

California law prescribes that blind students must spend a month in residence at the school while they are being trained to work with their new guides (this law does not exist in Michigan, where Dinah and Nelson's alma mater, Leader Dogs, is located, so Smitty and Tom were able to train on the outside). The dormitories provide custom-designed accommodations; there are twelve two-bed rooms, each with its own dog run, and a floor sink to provide drinking water for the dogs. I was intrigued to find that alternate doorknobs are different shapes, so that a blind student can recognize the right room.

It was time to head to the kennels, so we walked through a lovely inner park between the buildings, past a fragrance garden with plants labeled in Braille.

I didn't resist when they said we would start with the puppies, and it wasn't long before I had my arms full, from six-week-olds to twelve-weekers who were ready to be adopted out for their year of socializing. Over in a corner of the busy puppy department supply section was a closed-circuit television monitor keeping a constant surveillance on a yellow Labrador mother and her brand-new litter.

Guide Dogs breeds its own puppies at the organization's campus, outcrossing enough to keep the gene pool strong but maintaining a strict control standard to guard against hip dysplasia and other genetic problems to which these breeds are prone. To perpetuate the necessary qualities of intelligence and strength, those dogs who will produce the new generations of Guide Dogs are selected and bred with extreme care.

These chosen dogs, both males and females, do not live at the kennels but with families living within a fifty-mile radius of the school. When a female is due to be bred, she is brought back in for the three weeks she is in season. Her male friend is brought in for three days during that time. Then, following the mating, they both go back home. After two months, the female is brought in once again and settled in time to give birth to her babies. At the end of six weeks, her puppies weaned, home she goes until sometime in the future, when it is her turn again. This family orientation, like the 4-H socialization program, forestalls many of the personality problems that can occur with dogs raised in a kennel. Living with and serving humans is what these dogs are all about.

The breeding and whelping areas are rightfully off-limits to visitors, but thanks to TV we had a fine view of the yellow Lab and her babies without disturbing her. The seven nursing puppies all looked like pale little sausages, but in six weeks they would be weaned and ready for the serious business of puppy testing.

Now, at six weeks of age, each puppy begins its individual evaluation program. There is a most important underlying purpose to all this, but on the surface I must say there is an awful lot of fun to be had by all concerned.

Once a week for five weeks, the puppies are taken from the kennel one by one, cleaned and brushed, measured, weighed, and checked from stem to stern. There is no teaching involved at this stage, but for two hours trained observers—all volunteers—love and pet them while at the same time watching closely, taking careful notes on each puppy, then grading them on a scale from "poor" to "perfect."

The puppy activity is, to say the least, somewhat freeform: climbing up steps and—now, the hard way—coming back down, chasing a ball, trying to walk on a leash. Each one is checked for reactions to the unexpected—street grates, trash cans, cars approaching, even a starter's pistol. Are they outgoing and friendly or quiet and timid? Are they eager and curious or resistant? Are they crybabies? In this way, a comprehensive file—

a dossier, if you will—is compiled on each puppy that will be very important down the road when the time comes to match up, both in size and personality, the right dog with the right person.

When the puppies are around twelve weeks old, it is time for the next vital step. Each little one is given to a qualified young member of the local 4-H Club to be raised in a normal family environment for one year. There are certain ground rules. Everyone in the family must be completely agreeable to this program, the dog must live in the house with the family to learn good house manners, and there must be a fenced dog run or secure area outside.

Wearing the little green jackets that identify them as dogs in training, the puppies are accepted everywhere—department stores, markets, restaurants, sports events. Sometimes they even accompany their 4-H'er to school. There are some 725 in this program at any given time, and while it is the puppy who is learning about how to live productively in society, I have a hunch it's a two-way street.

At the end of the socializing year, the puppies are returned to the school, where they receive another thorough physical examination. Now comes very extensive testing to gauge their reactions to all sorts of situations they might be called upon to handle when they are responsible for a blind master or mistress. This is the most crucial evaluation period and leads into the next five difficult months of training. About half the dogs don't quite make it.

Parting with their dogs after such a close year is a tough hurdle for the 4-H youngsters and their families. The question is always "How can they possibly bear to do it?" These people are fully aware of this part of the bargain when they volunteer to take a puppy. One of the compensations that helps balance the heartache comes on graduation day. These moving ceremonies take place outdoors on the patio. After four hard weeks of training, all the blind students are seated with their dogs beside them. One by one, a name is called and the young puppy raiser comes forward and presents that dog, now fully trained, to the new master. The graduation is now official. There is tremendous pride and satisfaction in knowing they have helped launch a dog on its career in service. Very often the family will turn right around and take on a new adoptee to raise for a year.

In the event a dog is washed out of the program before graduation, the adoptive family has first priority to take the dog back into their home as a pet.

This was precisely the situation with Elsa. She had been raised by a family with four children who all adored her, but they had already started with another puppy trainee and couldn't accommodate both—which, of course, turned out to be Rudy and Stacey's good fortune.

Shortly after Elsa came to her new home, Rudy and Stacey received a warm and touching letter from her first adoptive family. Young Christie Baine wrote about Elsa's habits and games, about what a wonderful dog she was and how much they missed her, and she wrote about their new puppy trainee, Taylor. Stacey answered the letter, you can be sure, and they still exchange updates occasionally. In fact, on a recent visit to Los Angeles, the whole Baine family—mother and four youngsters—came to see Elsa in her new home. The consensus was that Elsa's career change had been a smashing success.

It should come as no surprise that our tour of the puppy wing that day took awhile. I'd probably still be there, but there was much more to see.

Don Frisk, class supervisor, drove us into San Rafael so that we could watch an actual training session in progress. A licensed instructor, Annie Lerum, was working a gorgeous young male golden retriever, Fjord, one of the fifteen dogs on her string, through a quiet residential section of town. Don parked the car and we got out to follow them, staying about half a block behind so we could observe without causing a distraction.

Fjord was within two weeks of completing his training and working beautifully. Suddenly, I heard a quiet "oh-oh" from Don, whose practiced eye had seen something I missed completely. Fjord had led Annie under a tree with a small overhanging branch well above Annie's head. It would not, however, have cleared someone six feet tall, and Annie couldn't let it go by. She stopped Fjord, showed him the branch, reinforcing with "See, Fjord, this is what you must watch for," and took him back to try again. Again, Fjord led her under the branch. Again, they stopped and while Annie kept pulling on the branch, she explained in a gentle but very firm voice that this was not acceptable.

Back they went, and this time it was a thrill to see Fjord lead her around the offending branch, taking her wide enough so that he not only cleared the overhang but allowed room for Annie to clear it as well. At my side, I heard *Nice* move!" from Don. I was more than a little impressed. That is a pretty subtle assessment to ask a dog to make.

Near the end of the session, Fjord made only one more small mistake: he crowded Annie a little too close to some bushes growing along the sidewalk. It was scarcely noticeable and something any of us may do ten times a day, but Fjord had to learn to do better if he was to be in charge of someone who couldn't see. Annie corrected him and took him back for another go at it, but in the meantime a woman pedestrian came into view, approaching from the opposite direction. Once again, it was exciting to see Fjord make his instant choice. He steered Annie equidistantly between the bushes and the woman, missing both. Nice move.

Earlier in the day, I had asked Jennifer where the trainers and instructors came from. I thought of Smitty when she said they were usually chosen from those who had worked with dogs in the military or in police work: sentry dogs, canine patrols, and so on. However, she added that more and more were coming right out of college, where they had majored in animal sciences. And one of the women trainers didn't fit into any of those categories; she had worked with dolphins before coming to Guide Dogs.

Fjord came up to us when he had finished his session and graciously accepted our congratulations before getting into Annie's car. I heard later that Fjord made it to graduation with flying colors.

Don and I proceeded into downtown San Rafael to observe a small group of students who were soloing with their dogs for the first time. There were instructors present, but they do not participate at this stage—a person/dog team must work its way out of any mistakes unaided. The instructors intercede only when a matter of safety is involved.

Both the people and the dogs were enjoying their newfound freedom to the hilt. They were going in and out of stores, shopping, buying snacks, comparing purchases, crossing streets—all independently. The shopkeepers are familiar with this training procedure and cooperate fully.

Tom had often explained that *he* was the one who had to know where they were going, and then the dog would get them there. So I realized that this happy new experience I was watching carried with it a tremendous challenge. All these people came from somewhere else. In addition to soloing with their dogs for the first time, they were in a strange city. They had only trained in San Rafael for a short period, so they were finding their way around town from a very limited memory. As amazing as these dogs are, they are no help when it comes to reading street signs.

Eventually, all the teams found their way back to the Guide Dog training lounge in the middle of town, to be driven back to school. I had to comment to Don on the variety of the people themselves.

He said, "It's typical. Each class will have members of both sexes. There will be different races and economic backgrounds."

It was astounding to see the giddy sense of camaraderie that prevailed, especially considering that up until a very short time ago the only thing these people had in common was blindness. I kept hearing "I did things I never believed *possible* without help!" and "I'll never touch my cane again." There was also a *lot* of hugging and wagging going on. This was a big day for both ends of the leash.

I wanted to get back to school in time to see "recess" period before I had to head for home. We made it with a few minutes to spare, which meant we just had time to see Dr. Craig Dietrich's fine veterinary hospital facilities on campus, complete with state-of-the-art equipment and dedicated medical personnel. Typically, here too was the resident four-legged staff member to show us around. In this case, she was an older German shepherd named Rolly, a retiree who had just never moved out.

As well as ministering to the dogs currently living at the school, the hospital is available to any graduate whose dog has a health problem. If a former student can bring his dog in, the dog receives medical care, free of charge, for life. Rolly let me see the tattoo on the inside of her ear, identifying her as a Guide Dog. All the puppies receive this at about eight weeks of age, and I assured Rolly it was a badge of honor.

As we headed back to the kennel area for playtime, I saw a funny tableau that is a little hard to describe. The large fenced outdoor exercise areas are separated by a passageway, perhaps twenty feet wide. Along one side, seated on the ground with their backs propped up against the wire fence, were three of the young handlers. Each one had a grown dog lying on its back in front of her with the dog's head resting in her lap. It was teeth cleaning time for two golden retrievers and one German shepherd, and everybody was very relaxed and content as the handlers continued to work on the dogs' mouths. What cracked me up was that, as we passed by, all three upside-down dogs began wagging their tails enthusiastically without changing position at all!

Seeing three of the ten guide dog schools firsthand had provided a great overview of the fine work being done in this field. As we waited for "recess" to start, Jennifer and Don filled me in on some interesting background. It came as a real surprise to learn that, for a variety of reasons, only between 2 and 5 percent of the blind obtain dogs. Some of these people have physical limitations, some are not able to maintain a dog in their living situation, and some are simply not interested in owning a dog at all. The cost of the program is certainly not a factor, because the schools are privately funded by interested parties. Some of the schools charge a minimal fee; most do not. At Guide Dogs, the blind receive their dogs, their training, room and board during that four-week period, plus yearly follow-up home visits by a field representative for the life of the dog—all without charge of any kind! Sponsorship of a dog from birth through training to graduation is $12,000.

At four o'clock, it was "recess" time at last. This is the period set aside every afternoon when the grown dogs are let out into the community play areas, some twenty or so big dogs to each large space. For about an hour, they are all free to interact with one another, romping and playing, tussling, forming friendships in groups of two or three or simply mingling, just being dogs. The trainers join in for this R and R session, happy to be playmates for a little while, rather than instructors. Small wonder that, over and over again, I kept hearing, "Betty, don't tell anybody, but I'd pay them to let me do this!" or "I'm never ready to go home at the end of the day!"

.   .   .

Finally I had to tear myself away and start back to Carmel. The fond goodbyes were genuine on both sides, and I knew we would see each other again.

The California summer twilight has always been a magic time for me—exhilaration laced with a drop of melancholy. Driving back through the rolling hills along the coastline, I had a lot to think about.

Guide Dogs for the Blind had come a long way from where it started in 1942—with one trainer and four donated German shepherds, one of whom came from the San Francisco dog pound. Their first class consisted of two students in a town called Los Gatos, which means "the Cats"! All that was six thousand dogs ago.

I found myself trying to imagine our Dinah as one of those new puppies—or, a little later on, as a schoolgirl. How many life-altering passages the Lady had gone through!

There were the first few weeks of babyhood spent with her litter brothers and sisters; the obligatory year with her 4-H family, learning about the outside world; back to school to give her heart to Smitty during her training period, as she learned her profession; and then the *big* change when she had to reclaim her heart in order to give it to Tom and her Sullivan family. And for Dinah it didn't end there. One more time, she had managed to reach out and include me in her circle of close ones.

If only I could acquire some of her remarkable ability to assimilate change!

When or how I got the idea of giving a Guide Dog for Christmas years ago is a little vague, but to me it seemed the ideal gift in the spirit of the season, as it is both people- and animal-oriented. I send personal notes each year explaining that together we are sponsoring a new Guide Dog, and as a result, their present is a little hard to wrap. It is the only gift I have ever found that always seems to fit.

And now, wonder of wonders, through totally unrelated circumstances, I had one of these phenomenal creatures of my very own.

Oh, yes. I had a lot to think about on that drive home.

Dinah's integrity and stamina, under any conditions, have long been her hallmark, and that same resilience holds her in good stead even today as a lady in retirement. She really should be giving classes in how to grow old gracefully.

Sometimes when we girls—and boys too, I'm sure—have reached a certain age, we find it takes a little more time to get our engines started each day. A few unfamiliar muscles seem reluctant to limber up.

The other morning, I awoke before the alarm and lay there in a cozy half doze for the few remaining minutes. In the dimness, I could see the big coppery mound that was the sleeping Dinah. As I watched, her even breathing changed rhythm; there were deep sighs now and then, and I became aware that her eyes had opened. She was doing exactly the same thing I was doing: slowly getting her act in gear for the day. Finally, with a grunt, she eased herself to her feet—just a beat before the alarm went off. It was slipper time.

Tom spoke earlier of feeling compelled to be the one who was never depressed because he felt he was the one asking people for help. I wonder if his companion of nine years might not subscribe to that same theory. Her immediate response is *always* cheerful and upbeat. Her tail starts to wag almost before her eyes are open.

There are certain nights when going up the stairs to bed seems more of an effort for Dinah, but no way is she going to be left out of the routine. On those nights, I no longer try to convince her that she would be better off downstairs.

It didn't take her long to teach me what to do. She would keep up a low, intermittent bark until I'd come back downstairs and find her standing with her feet on the first step, wagging her tail. All that was needed, I soon learned, was to put my hands under her hip bones for light support, and then the Lady charged up the steps as usual. She doesn't abuse this privilege, but makes it clear on the nights when my help would be appreciated.

As we know, it was Dinah's eyesight that first alerted Tom to the fact that his pal was losing some of her sharpness. Well, I am happy to report that the problem seems to have reached a plateau and has slipped no further. It is my little Timothy for whom the world is growing steadily darker. However, he still watches from his window-on-the-world on the stair landing and remains in charge of the Early Warning System. Tim can spot a crow alighting in the top of the pine tree a block away, but if anything is out of place on the floor, he's apt to walk into it. Does he mope about it? Not for a second.

Tim compensates. He takes shorter steps; his circus-pony gait is now more a mincing walk; entering a room where the light is not very bright, he tends to hug the wall. And evidently he seems to think he sees better sitting up, for I often walk into a room these days and find him sitting up in the middle of the floor, all by himself, for no apparent reason. Timmy is the only dog I've ever known who actually seems smaller when he's sitting up than when he's on all fours—but if it works for him, I'm all for it.

Above all, I must not let it make me sad. Regretful, yes, but to be sad when we're together would be a great disservice to a little guy who hasn't lost a drop of his enthusiasm or marvelous joie de vivre. It was another dear poodle friend who taught me that lesson. We lived together for five happy years after Dancer's lights went out completely. There is much to be learned from these friends if we only pay attention. Cataract surgery is available today for dogs as well as humans. Appropriate cases have met with success, but at Tim's age—well over the ten-year mark—an operation was not advised. The progressive dimming

is very gradual, and the doctor says he may retain enough minimal vision to last him for life.

Lady Dinah is so elegant it seems totally out of character to
broach such an indelicate subject as bodily functions. However, I
have often wondered how the blind person–dog team handles
some of the realities of life.

I can understand giving the dog regular opportunities to take
care of those necessities: first thing in the morning, after a meal,
bedtime—that's par for the course for anyone with a pet. But how
does a blind person know if his dog is having a problem? Without
getting too graphic, I can say that the cursory stool check is a way
of life for responsible pet owners. How does the person without
sight know when there might be an unscheduled call of nature?
I've come to believe the answer is simple. The dog says so.

Dinah made this clear one night after we had been together a
few months and had settled into our routines. After the last out at
bedtime, everybody treks upstairs for cookies while I get ready
for bed, a small puppy biscuit for each of the boys, a big one for
the redhead, *none* for the aging blonde. I break each biscuit into
three pieces so it will seem like three times as much. Their figures
mustn't go to pot any more than mine.

On this particular night, I was suddenly nudged awake around
4 A.M. Dinah wasn't at all tentative about it. Unlike the polite
morning slipper wake-up, this time it was an insistent "I need you
now! It's important!"

She let me find my own slippers, preceding me down the stairs
two at a time to the back door, where she anxiously waited for me
to shut off the alarm and unlock the door. I watched her through
the window, and she wasted no time getting busy.

Tom claimed to be able to tell by Dinah's breathing pattern
whether or not she had to go out, but I am not as astute. He had
also made a point of the fact that if Dinah woke up in the morning

before Tom was ready to rise and shine, he simply had to say, "Go back to sleep, girl," and she would be still as a mouse. I had tried that once or twice, when I could steal a few extra minutes, and found it worked like a charm (I must admit, I don't make a habit of this, as I can't help thinking how I would feel if the situation were reversed!). So this wee-small-hour gambit was particularly unusual for a dog who ordinarily was not to be heard from once she sacked out.

Eventually, not realizing she was being observed, she returned to the door and let out one muffled bark—literally, a stage whisper—and then sat and waited. I let a few moments go by to see how long it would take her to ask again, but she just sat there.

Needless to say, I blinked first. I let her in and she headed straight back to bed. Well, almost straight. There was a momentary detour as she checked to see if she could con me out of one more cookie. When she struck out on that, it was back to sleep for the night, and by morning everything was as usual.

Of course, Dinah would have been forgiven a mistake under emergency circumstances, but she is never one to take advantage of an easy shortcut; she gives everything her best shot. She has used that urgent nudge on a few occasions since, not just during the night but wherever I happen to be. I have learned that particular signal means only one thing, and I pay attention. She's not the only smart one in the house.

Curious to know how dogs are taught to be so dependable in that department, I knew the one to ask was Harold Smith. If Smitty doesn't know the answer to a question about dogs after twenty-five years of training them, it isn't worth your time.

When I called him, Smitty explained that dogs in training to be leaders of the blind are put on a strictly regimented time schedule and are taught to go in only two places, either the kennel or the "dog area." A Leader Dog is up by seven every morning and taken to the designated area to be walked on leash. "Park!" is the word commonly used, and it means "Get busy right now!" This procedure is repeated at given hours, three or, at most, four times a day. The person who ultimately receives his or her guide dog is encouraged to adhere to this schedule as closely as possible.

"It sounds simple enough, but"—I had to ask—"why wouldn't that apply to any dog, not just working dogs?"

"It does, of course," Smitty said, "but you have to really focus on the dog in the beginning until he gets the idea. Sighted people are easily distracted. They're in a hurry. They're thinking of a couple of other things at the time. Something catches their eye. They give up too soon, and the dog gets confused. People will paper the whole house and then wonder why their dog doesn't form good habits."

These strictly business exercise periods can be extended into playtime, of course, but not until the primary mission has been accomplished. A new blind master is taught to keep the health of the animal in mind at all times. Any irregularity or atypical behavior must be noted, and if it doesn't correct itself immediately, it should be brought to the attention of a veterinarian. Preventive health care is the watchword.

Shortly after Dinah came to live with me, I took her to see Dr. Ray Sprowl at Brentwood Pet Clinic, who has been doctoring my animals for thirty years. The visit was ostensibly to check the Lady out and transfer her medical records, but I cannot deny that I was bursting to show her off as well.

Ray agreed that she was gorgeous, naturally, but he was even more impressed by the fine condition she was in. When he turned her over for examination, she laid those broad hips flat on the floor like a young ballet dancer, with no sign of discomfort whatsoever.

Ray broke into a delighted grin. "If you only knew how few golden retrievers I examine who can do that at *any* age these days!" We both knew he was referring to the old nemesis of this beautiful breed, hip dysplasia. The golden's popularity, resulting in so much indiscriminate overbreeding, is only exacerbating the situation. Great news, indeed, to receive those encouraging words from Ray Sprowl.

Because Tom's work program—speeches, concerts, seminars—entails frequent travel, Smitty had given Dinah some additional adaptive training. She was taught that it was all right to go on various different surfaces, not only grass or dirt. On a quick break between planes, often tarmac is all that is available.

Tom says Dinah was a superb traveler. If she had to wait longer than usual, she could slow her breathing, lie very still, and sustain until she could be taken out.

He laughed. "Nelson, on the other hand, has to pee often, like men do. A five-hour cross-country flight is real tough for Nelson; he just can't get the mileage Dinah did. I often structure my flights with him through convenient airline terminals. In Atlanta, Delta courtesy cars can take Nels for a run. LAX has a grass area on the baggage level. Kennedy is good. Seattle is great. Dallas/Fort Worth is the best."

It wasn't all that convenient for Dinah, but then, it's always been trickier for girls.

Knowing she would be doing a great deal of traveling, Smitty had done a magnificent job in airport training with Dinah. She learned to find the baggage claim area by putting that sensitive nose in the air and sniffing it out, partly by the scent of the luggage but also by the smell of the outside air that comes in with the baggage carts. She learned not only how to ride an escalator but how to locate one by the smell of the grease used to lubricate the mechanism; ditto the moving sidewalk. It was also on her agenda to find the front desk in unfamiliar hotel lobbies.

Think of the choices and decisions that this dog was continually called upon to make. Yet she was invariably ready, willing, and eager to hit the road.

8
TOM

THINKING OF THE DAYS Dinah and I spent on the road to-gether is like watching a movie montage. So many different places, so many different scenes—not always in se-quence, but that's how memories are.

By the time I got Dinah, in late 1977, things had improved quite a bit. I was playing mostly major hotels, in places like Vegas, Reno, and Lake Tahoe, along with the summer theater circuit in lovely resorts such as Newport, Rhode Island, and Hyannis on Cape Cod. Even so, I wish the Lady could describe the difference between the preparation she experienced dur-ing her training and real life as it was in her early travel days with me.

Once we got through our initial shakedown cruise, Dinah and I became loving road companions. She not only coped, she prospered. Travel was always exciting to her, and she was al-ways eager to get on the way.

She really began to comprehend my system. We often traveled with David Foran, who was my road manager. Dinah understood that when I gave speeches she would wait for us in the room. She knew it when David or I was prepared to take her out on walks. Based on the clothes I was putting on, she seemed to figure out whether we were doing concerts, going to play golf, headed for a day of business, or going for a run.

From the outset, Dinah always tried to do what was expected of her, even if she was not absolutely sure what that was. She was ready to tackle any problem, great or small. As it happened, one of the earliest situations involved something "great."

I had been hired to perform at a nightclub called the Nugget in Reno, Nevada. It was my first big job. I was more than a little excited about that—and about opening for what was then the hottest comedy act in show business, Dan Rowan and Dick Martin, who had starred in the TV show *Laugh In*. I was scared to death.

At the Nugget Hotel, over the past twenty years, there has been a rather special opening act. This is the remarkable elephant, Bertha, who has been pleasing audiences for two shows a night, seven days a week, during all that time. I want to say right here and now that I love elephants, and during my two weeks at the Nugget, Bertha and I became good friends. But on my opening night, I was unaware of one important thing about elephants.

An elephant can move its multi-ton body in total silence. I mean *total* silence, so quietly that even a blind person wouldn't hear Bertha moving around the stage. Well, that tickled Dick Martin's funny bone and gave him an idea. He thought it would be terrific to surprise me on my opening night by involving Bertha in my act.

Dinah and I were backstage, waiting for my entrance cue,

and I told Dinah to lie down and stay still while I gave my performance. She was used to that; it happened all the time.

In those days, the music I used for beginning my show was a popular song called "I Can See Clearly Now," which I thought was an extremely appropriate description of how I viewed life. The orchestra began my introduction. I went onstage—and so did the silent Bertha. Dick had arranged for the trainer to sneak Bertha up behind me. As I began to sing "Look all around, nothing but blue skies, look straight ahead, nothing but blue skies," the trainer said, "Bertha! Trunk up!"—and the next thing I knew I was twelve feet in the air.

What I remember most is not the feeling of suddenly being up on Bertha's head but the sound of Dinah trying to decide whether to howl or growl at this moving, living building that was carrying her master away. She broke the "stay" rule and came onstage.

As I continued to sing, Dinah was using every vocal sound in *her* repertoire. The fact that she was challenging an elephant didn't faze the Lady; she wanted me down where I belonged!

It was our biggest number ever, but Dinah and I both opted not to keep it in the act.

There were the small things, too.

When Blythe was eight years old, what she wanted above all else was a Maltese puppy. Planning a special surprise on Christmas Eve, Dinah and I flew over to Las Vegas to the home of a wonderful family who raised these special little dogs and found Season.

A Maltese puppy weighs about a pound and a quarter, if that. She was so tiny, I decided to carry her home. So picture the scene: Dinah, leading me through the Las Vegas airport, and arriving at the security check with me, holding Season in my hand; an efficient security woman at the checkpoint trying to do her job while attempting to sort out why a blind man was using one dog to work while he was carrying another. I remember telling her Season was a guide dog in training, which I thought was pretty funny, but it did not register with the security guard.

I finally got both dogs onto the airplane, then home, and need I tell you it was a very special Christmas morning in our house?

Young Dinah thought the puppy was hers and wanted to play with her. On about the third or fourth morning, she accidentally stepped on Season's paw and broke it. Season healed quickly but Dinah was really upset; she was afraid Season was mad at her. She was very careful around the puppy from then on, and Season has been the boss ever since.

Then there are the times something happens that makes you feel like such a jerk you can't believe you could be so insensitive to the physical well-being of your animal.

I had been hired by Danny Thomas, along with a group called Sister Sledge, to perform at the Starlight Theater in Kansas City in August 1979. Now, folks, August in Kansas City is hot. How hot *was* it? Well, during my ten-day run, the average daytime temperature was around 100 degrees, with a humidity dew point almost as high.

Our performance was scheduled for eight o'clock each night, as the sun was setting. I think the Starlight is one of the largest outdoor theaters in America, with a seating capacity of around 10,000. The stage seemed to be the size of a football field; it was at least forty yards from the wings to where my piano was located.

We had arrived in Kansas City at about ten o'clock the night before our performance, and I spent a couple of hours before going to bed teaching Dinah to take me from the wings to the baby grand piano in the center of the stage. After a number of efforts, she got the idea, and she took a great deal of pride in getting me exactly to the piano bench.

The stage surface was some kind of hardwood, probably maple; wood is one of those materials that heats up to the point at which it even blisters. It hadn't entered my mind to consider the problems the heat might make for Dinah's sensitive paws. I have heard that animals have much higher thresholds of pain than we do—maybe we think that because they don't have the ability to use language to tell us.

Opening night arrived, and Danny Thomas was on the stage talking about "This fresh new blind singing talent, Tom Sullivan," he was about to introduce. The night before when I worked with Dinah, I encouraged her to cross the stage slowly, in order to milk the audience. When Danny Thomas said "Ladies and gentlemen, Tom Sullivan!" Dinah was given the command "Forward" and moved easily out from the wings onto the stage—except that what was supposed to be a sedate walk to the piano became a forty-yard dash. Dinah leaned forward into the harness and sprinted her way across the stage. I was nearly pulled off my feet. I couldn't understand it.

I got to the piano in no time flat, so I had to stand and wait for quite a while in order for the orchestra to get to my introductory music. My performance was a rousing success: two standing ovations. I was ecstatic! At the end, as I stood at the piano to take my bows, I could feel Dinah yanking on my hand to leave the stage. After acknowledging the audience, I turned to leave and, once again, the forty-yard dash began. As I reached the safety of the shaded area, I leaned down and said, "Dinah, what the hell are you doing? What's the matter with you, girl?"

We went back to the hotel, but neither Dinah nor I could sleep. I was wired with the excitement of the evening, and Dinah was constantly licking her paws. The sound really got to be annoying. "Cut it out!" I said, in a voice much too harsh. The licking continued. "Dinah," I said irritably, "what's the matter with you?" Still, the licking went on, and then, finally, Dinah gave in to her pain and whimpered. I thought she needed to go outside again. "Okay, girl, let's go," I said, but Dinah didn't move. "Come on, girl," I said. "I'll take you out." Again, Dinah didn't move. I got nervous, now. I went to her. She was breathing fast and still licking at one of her paws. I reached over to touch it, and she yelped in pain. All four of the golden girl's paws were scorched. The pads must have literally burned through. I was horrified. In an instant I realized what had happened. Telling her to stay still, I called room service for buckets of ice. For the rest of the night, I sat on the floor and rubbed her blistered pads with ice cube after ice cube, until my hands were nearly frozen solid.

The ice did help. By the next day, although she couldn't work, Dinah could walk, and within ten days the resilient golden girl had recovered completely. It had been a learning experience for me, but what a price the Leading Lady had to pay!

The Lady and I had a variety of exciting times on the road during the three years I spent working for *Good Morning America* as a special correspondent. In that time, David often didn't travel with us, and Dinah was forced to take on all the responsibility. We flew over a million miles in those three years and covered stories ranging all the way from small towns, where we might interview one of America's true heroes—perhaps a person conquering a disability—to high-profile celebrities in elegant surroundings. Those times that I was assigned to cover boxing for GMA, I dragged Dinah into sweaty locker rooms and training gyms, where we talked with such people as Sugar Ray Leonard, Roberto Duran, Muhammad Ali, and Larry Holmes.

The assignment to cover Muhammad Ali's preparation for his last fight, with Larry Holmes, at his Deer Lake training camp in Pennsylvania, was memorable for more reasons than one.

I was getting ready to meet the champ for the first time and had let Dinah out for a moment of peace and quiet before we went to Muhammad's training facility. When my good friend and producer, Susan Winston, arrived with her husband, Jim, I walked outside the hotel room to call Dinah back to get ready for work. As she always did, she responded immediately to my call and came bounding up to me. I heard a gasp from Susan and Jim, and then I felt it. Usually silky-coated Dinah had a slimy, gooey, sticky substance all over her thick fur. Dinah must have discovered a gusher, or the neighborhood oil slick, for she was completely covered in grungy black guck! I didn't know what to do. We had to be at the champ's training camp in less than an hour, and somehow we had to get the Lady clean.

Jim found the hotel maid's cart and commandeered half a dozen tiny bottles of shampoo. What a commercial they missed! The golden girl in a tub full of water, flooded with Prell. She hated it, I hated it, the Winstons hated it, and I'm sure the hotel hated it when they tried to get Dinah's red hair out of the drain. It was not one of our finest hours.

However, the girl cleaned up pretty good, as they say, and when we arrived at our interview with Muhammad Ali, Dinah was the star of the camp. I can truly say that when I saw him again, years later, Muhammad remembered Dinah much better than he remembered me.

In the last ten years this nation has clearly awakened to the needs of people dealing with disabilities. Whether it is accessible bathrooms or wheelchair ramps, improved telecommunications for the deaf, talking computers, or Braille placed on the inside of elevators, signifying the particular floors, recognition of the special needs of the disabled has increased 1,000 percent.

In the early days with the Leading Lady, however, this business of Braille floor numbers hadn't been worked out. So usually, when we got on an elevator, I waited until other people were boarding with us, asked them to punch our floor, and hoped they hit the right button.

Once we got off those elevators, Dinah was uncanny at finding my room. But I gave her a little help, too. I always left the television going and placed a rubber band on the doorknob, so I could identify the room before I stuck a key in the lock. (Marking the doorknob was a holdover from my Harvard days, when we would use a man's tie to indicate the presence of a girl or girls in our rooms.)

I remember one night when things didn't quite work according to plan, and Dinah and I found ourselves in a very odd predicament. We were in the Anatole Hotel in Dallas, Texas.

The Anatole is extremely large. I'm not sure how many rooms, but at least fifteen hundred, and it has to be eighteen stories in height. On this night we tried to make it alone back to our room, after Dinah's late walk. But with no one else in the elevator, it became a question of trial and error. Push a button and remember where it was in the row of buttons. The elevator door would open and I would say, "Good girl, find the room, find the room," and then I'd feel her look up at me as if I had lost it. You see, Dinah knew every time whether we were on the right or wrong floor. Her nose told her that. How did she handle it? In typical Leading Lady style. Each time, since all the doors looked alike, she would take me to the room that most identified in location to our own.

Boy, did we have some interesting moments! From having a very angry man fling his door open at the sound of my key in the lock, expecting a burglar, to interrupting a couple at an in-

© CRAIG STUDIO OF PHOTOGRAPHY

Allen and me outside stage entrance to the Cape Playhouse in Dennis, Massachusetts, around the time we met Tom Sullivan.

With Pyewacket, Allen's and my co-star in *Bell, Book, and Candle*.

Tom in rehearsal, around the same time.

Dinah's first meeting with the Sullivans, at the Marriott Hotel in Detroit, 1977.

Tom, Dinah, and Smitty in front of the Leader Dogs office,
Detroit, 1978.

The Sullivans then—

—and now.

Tom performing on *Kelly & Company.*

. . . with Dinah at his feet.

On the bike
path.

On the beach.

Riding.

Waterskiing.

Golfing with Patty.

Zooing with Mookie (and Laurie Middleton).

Tom finishing in the Tom Sullivan 10K race held annually in Torrance, California. The proceeds benefit blind children.

AT WINTER PARK.

Tom and Blythe, his ski guide.

Patty and me about to board the Snocat.

Sully and Nelson.

Tom with the rest of
the gang: Nelson,
Season, and Cay,
1990.

My family: Timothy,
Cricket, Dinah . . .

. . . and the elusive T.K.
who is definitely *not* in show
business. 1990.

Reunion.

timate moment, to being invited in by a bunch of overzealous partyers, to waking up two Japanese businessmen who did not understand English. We spent over two frustrating hours walking around from floor to floor in the Anatole. But the Lady never quit trying. And I'm grateful that I didn't let my frustration carry over into the way I worked her. This time I stayed patient and eventually, through the process of trial and error, we got back to our own room.

Do you wonder why I didn't return to the lobby and ask for help? I certainly would do that today. I suppose it was this business of seeking true independence. Tom Sullivan, in the early days with the Leading Lady, was truly Mr. Macho. It was probably my version of the family out for the Sunday drive. You know the ride I mean—where the father gets lost but will *not* pull into a gas station to check a map or ask for directions. I hope this is as close as I come to that odd form of American male pigheadedness.

In her travels, what did Dinah eat? Well, guide dogs are supposed to be kept on a completely balanced diet. Dinah thrived on her morning and evening meal of Science Diet, a product that was developed largely through the efforts of the Morris Animal Foundation. But on the rare occasions that I was unable to obtain her regular food, I would resort to emergency measures. One of her most unappetizing meals consisted of two boxes of Kellogg's cold cereal, usually Rice Krispies, served with warm water gravy over the top, along with two very rare hamburgers from some fast food joint, all crunched together, which she seemed to enjoy.

There were other nights, to be sure, when we accepted the kindness of a restaurateur here or there in America, who wanted to give Dinah the best filet mignon he had in the place. She also, on occasion, ate baked potato and chicken—no bones, of course. I guess I believed that if I could eat it, she could eat it. Sorry, Dinah. I'm sure there were some nights you would have loved some Pepto-Bismol or Alka-Seltzer.

Then there were the restaurants who didn't want us inside their establishments at all. As most of you know, a law protects the rights of blind people to bring working dogs into any place serving food. But self-important maître d's and people from other countries are not always up on constitutional law. We have had our problems, and I haven't necessarily always handled them well.

Once, Dinah and I were ejected from a restaurant in New York called Mortimer's. In trying to explain the situation to the owner, I had reached the stage of exasperation just this side of the point of no return, when it occurred to me that, rather than deck him, there was a more effective way to make my point. The next morning, on *Good Morning America,* I convinced my bosses to let me editorialize. I explained that, by law, working dogs were not pets but necessary co-workers and had earned the right to go anywhere. Two months later, when Dinah and I returned to Mortimer's, we sat at a front table, where Dinah was personally welcomed by the owner and hand-fed a treat.

The Lady's modes of transportation were even more diverse: limos, buses, trucks, even a covered wagon, and, in the air, everything from a 747 to a Piper Cub. She took them all in stride—with one exception.

In the attempt to make three appearances on one particular summer day, David and I leased a helicopter, which landed on the roof of our hotel. We then suggested to Dinah that she climb in and enjoy the flight.

The howl she let out would have rivaled anything from *Call of the Wild.* Imagine her fear, looking out into empty space as this vehicle of man's creation rose straight into the air off the roof of a building. Marriages have probably ended over less dramatic moments.

One ever-present problem was the thoughtless people who would pull, maul, paw, and nearly mutilate the beautiful golden girl. Because her face is so sensitive and her personality so doe-like, people immediately felt they could pat her at any time. Maybe the oddest example of this kind of behavior was a man who saw Dinah and me getting ready to enter a revolving door. He rushed across the lobby of the hotel and thrust himself in the door with us. The three of us struggled to keep the door moving forward, while he lassoed Dinah around the neck with a bear hug, telling her, "Good girl. What a nice golden retriever!" Dinah and I cleared the door, while he nearly got knocked out cold as it came around, hitting him in the back of the head. Maybe it knocked some sense into him.

Let me make the point once again. Guide dogs are working animals. They are *not* pets. There is nothing wrong with showing affection toward them, *if* you ask the master and *if* the harness is down and the dog is not working. But grabbing, groping, clutching, and grasping is not playing the game according to the rules. The best analogy I can give has to do with the way men treat women in the workplace. With the growth in awareness of the rights of women today, it would be highly unlikely that a male would pinch a girl on the derriere while she was walking through a crowded office, just because he wanted to. The same concept applies in dealing with working dogs. They are working—it's that simple.

Dinah, always a great icebreaker, was at her best when we interviewed handicapped children. It was as if she knew the kids had some sort of disability, and if possible she became even softer and more gentle, letting them crawl all over her. This openness of canine spirit allowed me to ask all kinds of questions that kept the interviews positive and caring. Such was the case with the Sunshine Kids, an organization based in Houston, Texas, that works to fulfill special requests from children who are dealing with catastrophic diseases. This group provides the Sunshine Winter Games, held in Colorado each year, and *Good Morning America* sent me to cover those games.

Meeting children battling to stay alive, and yet loving life with a passion, made me realize that no one's problem, most particularly my ongoing war with blindness, could be thought of as significant when mirrored against the life-and-death issues faced by these remarkable children.

The little girl who most took my heart with her sense of joy and enthusiasm was named Molly Newberry. When I met Molly the first year, she was sick with cancer but still healthy enough to participate with gusto in all the events of the Winter Games. On the second night she asked me if Dinah could sleep in her room. The golden girl had no objection, and neither did I; and so, with their mutual loving gentleness, a remarkable bond was formed. Over the next few days, Dinah would follow Molly around, not even worrying about whether I needed her to work. After the games were over and Molly went home, she wrote often, rarely asking how I was but always demanding news of Dinah's exploits.

The next year, when I returned to the Winter Games, Molly had gone through the ravages of her illness. Both legs had been removed above the knee, and Molly was wheelchair bound. At their winter dance, Molly asked if I would dance with her.

"Just pick me up," she said. "We'll do all right."

As I held this little person in my arms and danced awkwardly around the floor, Molly said, "Tom, last night I had a dream."

"Oh?" I said. "What kind?"

"The angels told me it was just about time for me to go and live with them."

I hope I kept dancing.

"What did you tell them?" I asked.

"That I wasn't quite ready yet. That I had to finish the Winter Games."

The next day, Molly, Dinah, and I made the ugliest snowperson anybody had ever seen, with Dinah sticking her nose in, or choosing to lie in the snow, right in the way of our construction. Molly kept warm by putting her arms around the Leading Lady and hugging her close. Dinah loved it.

The following morning, when it was time for the Sunshine Kids to get back on the bus and head home to Texas, Molly said, "I love you, Tom. You're my wonderful friend."

I said mockingly, "You mean I'm not your best friend, Molly?"

"No," she said. "Dinah is my best friend." I had no trouble coping with the loving honesty of that special little girl.

Molly died a month later. Her angels did come for her, but I like to think that the Leading Lady had taken away some of her pain.

Not long after that, Dinah was able to communicate with a vastly different group of kids. This time, *Good Morning America* sent me to cover a group of problem juveniles who were participating in the Outward Bound Program. The idea was to place these kids, literally, in a nineteenth-century American wagon train moving west across the country.

These young people—actual felons, having committed serious crimes—were now being exposed to discipline coupled with constant support of their feeling of self-worth, while surrounded by the beauty of nature. It was a unique approach toward rehabilitation.

In this case, the group was headed for Portland, Oregon, from Kansas City. Dinah and I caught up with them in the Painted Desert of Arizona, and from the minute Dinah arrived, she was the hit of the trip. It was an experience to watch the kids handle the horses and the oxen, set up camp, serve the meals, and generally function as pioneers.

When we moved along during the day, I rode on the lead wagon with the wagon master and Dinah trotted along beside me, ranging into the sagebrush, coming across creatures she had never seen before in her whole city-oriented life. At night she was more than ready to curl up with one of the kids.

I, on the other hand, was not quite such a happy camper. I am not someone who likes to sleep on the hard ground under the western sky, wondering if some varmint I can't see is going to crawl into my sleeping bag. But the experience was worth it.

The interviews I did with the kids spoke to all of the contemporary issues confronting our nation that deal with children in trouble.

Environment does condition human beings, and the common frame of reference among these children was distrust for anyone in authority—parents, teachers, employers, law enforcement people. Many of these kids felt they had gotten a bad rap. Our wagon train was loaded with a number of young martyrs who felt sorry for themselves, but seeing Dinah work for me, with her unconditional love, sure didn't do them any harm.

A letter I received a month after that story had been on the air summed it up best. It was from a boy named Julian Brown, who I knew had been in and out of reformatories over the last four years, mostly for car theft, once for armed robbery. For him, this trip represented the end of the line. The next misstep would mean real prison as an adult, with hard-core convicts. His letter didn't make any long-range promises, but it did say this: "Dear Mr. Sullivan, thanks for talking to me on *Good*

Morning America—thanks for letting me get to know Dinah. It made me happy just to watch her and you. I wish I had a dog like that. But in my neighborhood, a dog just wouldn't work out. If you're ever in Chicago, here's my address on the South Side. Give me a call. You're a great dude, and so is your dog." And he signed the letter, "Peace."

Certainly not all of Dinah's adventures were related to *Good Morning America*.

There was the time Patty and I were going skiing with some friends at a resort where we decided it would be impractical to bring the Lady. At the end of our trip, however, I very much wanted Dinah to join me for the continuation of a concert tour, and I admit I took advantage of the airlines.

David Foran wears very heavy glasses that look like prescription sunglasses. Wearing these, and with Dinah in harness and working, he took the Leading Lady onto a United Airlines flight that would connect with me in Denver. This was much simpler than all the time and paperwork that would have been involved to enable anyone other than the dog's owner to bring the dog aboard.

Everything went perfectly until David was on the airplane and the 747 was in the air. Then he forgot himself. As Dinah rested comfortably on the floor, David picked up a newspaper and began to read. If Dinah could have understood what he was saying to the flight attendant, I am sure she would have considered his excuse lame-brained and embarrassing. But, thank goodness, the plane was off the ground, and she and David arrived safely to continue my tour.

And how about those times when even the refined Lady had to relieve herself in the middle of a busy show-business day?

Now, understand that Dinah would accommodate me in a planter box or on a newspaper or anywhere else I chose. Her whole philosophy was "Be elegant, private, quick, and efficient." But when we found ourselves on the set of M★A★S★H at 20th Century-Fox, for a hard week of taping, there wasn't a blade of grass or a private area to be found.

Dave and I wandered around sets, looking for some possibility, and then we found it. In an area used as an outdoor garden setting for one of the nighttime soap operas, there were huge boulders, literally the size of any rock found in the Colorado mountains. But of course these were fake, placed there by a creative set designer. One of these boulders was at least twelve feet across and fifteen feet high but couldn't have weighed more than fifty pounds. I will never forget Dave and me lifting this gigantic phony rock and encouraging Dinah to use the space it had occupied; like all good troupers, she followed directions without hesitation. We then covered the incriminating evidence by replacing the boulder and left the scene of our crime.

Dinah granted me freedom at every turn, but if I were to single out the one example that was most meaningful to me, it would have to be our trip to Scituate.

Scituate is a small seacoast town about twenty-eight miles south of Boston. It's where I grew up.

Twenty-five years later, after the death of my father, my mother chose once again to live in Scituate, and she bought a house only two blocks from where our home had been. The first time I visited her, I had an experience with Dinah I shall never forget.

I was on a business trip to Boston and decided to have my driver bring Dinah and me down to stay with Mom for a couple of days. As we neared the town, I could actually smell it. I wish I could break that smell down for you, but I can't. I just know that I could smell Scituate, and a funny excitement began to rise up in my stomach.

The first thing I did was stop at our old cottage. It had been sold a number of times and I didn't even know who lived in it now. I got out with Dinah and walked all over the property, even up to the front door, knocking and asking if I could come inside just to get the feel of it again. The family who now occupied it couldn't have been kinder, but I have to say it was because the Leading Lady was along.

They had two little children who just loved her to death. She didn't seem to mind at all, although she became a little concerned when I climbed the apple tree in the backyard. Yes, I did! I climbed the apple tree, sat up in the very top, picked an apple, and ate it, just like I had done when I was a child.

How I remembered sitting in this same tree. In my childhood, Scituate was a "lace curtain town," the place where Irish politicians came to vacation. My father, affectionately named Porky Sullivan, ran Irish pubs throughout Boston. On a weekend, I never knew who might be sitting on our porch, from Rocky Marciano or Ted Williams to John Hynes, the mayor of Boston. Our home was a hubbub of Irish conversation.

Against this backdrop of emotional enthusiasm, and sometimes turmoil, a blind child was trying to grow up and find a way to share his life with sighted children. While my mother worked hard to teach me the things I needed to know about cleanliness and manners, my father seemed to be one of those ebullient characters who believed there is a solution to any problem. He thought he could solve my childhood dilemma of friendships in his own unique way.

One night at about 3 A.M. Dad arrived home with Beansy Thornton, an ex-jockey—and an old, somewhat beaten down racehorse named Tucker's Boy that my father had won in a late-night card game.

That horse may have been older and slower than he used to
be, and he might not have been a special Thoroughbred to
others, but for me he was Black Beauty, Fury, My Friend
Flicka, the Black Stallion, and Trigger all rolled into one. I
called him Tuckey.

Even though it was against the city ordinances to have a
horse, and even though we didn't have the land to keep this
hay-eating animal, my father was determined that his blind son
would have a chance to become special in the neighborhood.
So next morning he was out on our front lawn with a very
large bell, like the town criers of old, ringing it and calling out,
"Sullivan's pony rides. Twenty-five cents apiece!" The kids
came from everywhere, and for the brief time the city let us
keep Tuckey, our home became the center of the neighborhood
for every Scituate child.

After that, each day, I wondered if the kids would show up
to play. I would stand in my backyard, listening to the sounds
of the neighborhood and hoping that either John or James or
Jackie would show up to spend the day with me. You see, they
had the option of going somewhere else if they wanted to, but I
couldn't just join them. Although my life was good, there
were many days when I stood in my yard waiting for a child to
arrive, listening to the sounds of the neighborhood, just as I
could hear them now. . . .

I finished my apple and climbed down from the tree.

I'd made a decision. I only had one bag, so I had the car leave
me there. I would walk to my mother's home. I knew exactly
where her house had to be, and I knew Dinah could get me
there.

My God, it was easy! I remembered just how all the streets
came together. The only thing that seemed a little distorted was
the distance—what used to be a long walk for short legs, we
now seemed to eat up in one third of the time.

My mother was shocked when Dinah and I arrived without

anyone helping us, but I was so full of life I think she got the idea. I bet it made her feel good to see her independent son with the Leading Lady.

After a good night's sleep and one of my mother's Irish breakfasts—three fried eggs, half a pound of bacon, sourdough toast, orange juice, milk, and a couple of chocolate doughnuts from the local bakery thrown in—it was time for Dinah and me to have an adventure, and what a day we had!

I told my mother I would go get her the morning paper. So Dinah and I walked the half mile along Scituate Avenue to Joe Thornton's store. Now, Joe Thornton had been in that store for at least forty years, and when I came in he greeted me in typical New England fashion, as if I had never been away. "Tom Sullivan, how are ya? I saw your mother the other day. She looks real good, doesn't she?" He never expected me to comment. He just kept rattling on. "How about those Red Sox, Tom? Haven't changed since you've been here, have they? Still in last place. What can I do for you this morning?" I said I needed a quart of milk and the *Boston Globe*, a couple of loaves of bread, and some orange juice. He provided them immediately. "Say hello to your mother for me and tell her I'll see her at church." "Thanks, Joe," I said, and Dinah and I moved along.

Next, just because I felt like it, I visited Tom O'Neill's sporting goods store, my favorite place in Scituate Harbor. You could still smell Wilson baseball gloves on the racks, and real leather NFL footballs. The brine of fishing tackle and the fresh bait locker dominated the smell most of all, and the talk of the men was singularly about sports.

There was one thing Dinah and I still had to achieve before our day ended.

When you stand on Scituate Beach and listen closely, you can hear the sound of a bell buoy ringing off the end of Scituate Harbor Point. It sounded the same as I remembered. Between the shore and the bell buoy, in a straight line about three hundred and fifty yards from the beach, was a small rock outcropping called Great Island. It was the place where neighborhood kids used to play Huck Finn and Tom Sawyer or Treasure Island, if they had the courage to swim out to the rock. I had never been there, because my mother wouldn't allow it. I think I was the only Scituate kid who had never set foot on Great Island, and as a thirty-five-year-old person, in 1982, I was committed to complete this childhood adventure.

It's funny how you never actually grow up. When I brought my parcels home from Joe Thornton's, I did the same thing I would have done had I had the courage when I was ten years old and wanted to go to Great Island: I lied to my mother. I just said I was going down to the beach to get some sun.

When Dinah and I arrived on the sand, almost everyone else had gone home. It was late in the afternoon, but the sun was still wondrously warm. Now, swimming is something that Dinah could do far better than I could. I am sure it is genetic in her golden retriever background, and since she had arrived in California, she and I had often taken morning swims—long ones.

Something I had forgotten, however, was that the water in New England is some 20 degrees colder than in southern California. A big change! An interesting thing about swimming in cold water is that when you are a little boy, the water never seems too bad, but as you get older it gets colder, and this water was definitely cold. I remembered wishing I had the luxurious coat of the golden girl. For her, this was just a cooling off after the hot afternoon sun.

The other thing I had forgotten was how strong the current was, not strong enough to endanger me but clearly strong enough to move me off course. As I swam out from the shore, the sound of the bell buoy seemed to move around. When I was on the beach, I was sure I knew exactly what the line was, but as I got farther from the shore, I wasn't so sure. The Atlantic surf doesn't crash in like it does in California, so when you are one hundred or two hundred yards from where you began, the sound of the beach cannot be heard. I was literally swimming blind and, now, somewhat deaf. I didn't panic, but I sure began to talk to the Leading Lady. "Hey, Dinah, what do you think? Where's the shore?" I started to use the kind of language that I learned during training. "Inside, Dinah. Find the step, Dinah." Anything I could think of that would jar her brain into realizing that I needed her help. I then reached out with my left hand and took her collar, literally letting her guide me in the ocean. She seemed to get the idea. She stopped swimming momentarily. Her head came up and she looked around and then, I'm not kidding, she actually licked my face and began to swim with those retriever power strokes toward, yes, what turned out to be Great Island.

I give you my solemn word as an Irish storyteller, I am not exaggerating. The Leading Lady found Great Island. And what a thrill! We had achieved Great Island. Wow!

We lay in the afternoon sun together, one of us drying and the other one shaking. One of the few unfortunate habits of golden retrievers is that with that big coat, they shake—often. Dinah kept showering me occasionally, but it felt just fine.

The swim back was easy. All we had to do was let the waves take us in the right direction. We arrived back on the beach, and I actually gave myself a hand. Bravo to me, I thought, and then I remembered who had allowed me to achieve my goal. I hugged Dinah with all the gratitude I could convey.

That night, my mother and I had those only–in–New England fried clams for dinner. Dinah tried one and turned the rest down. Who needed clams? We'd made it to Great Island!

There were highs and lows that the Lady and I experienced in our years of travel together, but one frightening experience seemed to encompass them all.

Dinah and I loved New York. It was the place, surprisingly, where we felt the most independent: where the skills we had developed over the years seemed to find their best use. For us, New York was the most special place we traveled to—until one June afternoon.

It was customary for me to walk Dinah four times a day, morning, noontime, at about five o'clock, and before we went to bed. The Carlyle Hotel, where we always stayed, is at 76th Street and Madison Avenue on the Upper East Side of Manhattan. It is truly one of America's most gracious, elegant, and, I have to admit, opulent hotels. Bobby Short and George Shearing, Mel Torme, and other jazz greats entertain nightly in the Crystal Café, and there is a wonderful low-key ambiance to the entire establishment. It also happens that most of the employees are Irish and have worked at the Carlyle for over thirty years. Many of them have become special friends of mine, and all of them loved the Leading Lady.

One day, Dinah and I headed out for one of our walks. As I said good afternoon to Jack, the doorman, he asked if I could wait just a moment and from deep inside his uniform jacket pocket emerged dog biscuits, brought from home just for the Lady. It's not appropriate to feed a guide dog during work time, but this was a special occasion.

After Dinah's gourmet delight, we started off along 76th Street to the first crossing, Madison Avenue, one of New York's busiest thoroughfares. People often ask me if guide dogs can see stoplights. That is to say, do guide dogs understand color? The answer is, they do not. Though they are not actually colorblind and can understand some shades, dogs do not have graphic color perception. When a guide dog assists a master across a busy street, the decisions are based on the flow of traffic more than the signal lights. Dinah's sense of judgment was simply the best ever. She knew that when the traffic moved over my left shoulder along 76th Street, she could cross Madison Avenue, and in the years we traveled to New York, the Lady never made a mistake. She even became sensitive to the idea that taxicabs were apt to turn the corner on yellow, a behavior that can drive any pedestrian, sighted or blind, crazy.

Continuing down 76th, Dinah and I strolled along the tree-lined sidewalk with beautiful brownstone houses towering to our right. It is a magnificent part of New York.

Our next crossing was Fifth Avenue. Dinah achieved the goal easily and entered her sanctum, Central Park. I have always let Dinah run in the park. She loved to chase squirrels, and often I would bring a tennis ball and enjoy a lively game of catch with the golden girl. My rule was to never allow Dinah to move beyond my ability to hear the sound of her collar.

On this day, however, even the Leading Lady wasn't perfect. A squirrel came just too tantalizingly close, prompting her to bound after it, moving her just out of the collar-sound range. When I called her, I'm sure she responded immediately. But a phenomenon of any large city occurred. My voice, the thing that bound us together, bounced off massive buildings and large trees, creating for Dinah a false sense of where my call was coming from.

Both of us panicked. I screamed, "Dinah! Dinah! Come here, girl. Come on, girl, let's go home. Come on, girl!" And Dinah, not knowing where I was, did the only thing she could think of. As I learned afterward from Jack, the doorman, Dinah headed on a dead run for the Carlyle Hotel. This time she did not consider traffic laws, and she arrived at the Carlyle much sooner than I did.

My trip back to the hotel was far more harrowing. I now became absolutely, totally blind. Where once the Leading Lady and I moved easily along the elegant tree-lined street, now, with my hands straight out in front of me, I tried to grope my way back to the hotel. And, though I hate to say it, not one New Yorker tried to help me.

Listening to the sound of other pedestrians, I made the cross-ings of Fifth, and then Madison, without injury. And there it was: the sound of Dinah's collar, and then her feet. She raced the 150 yards from the Carlyle along 76th Street, literally leap-ing into my arms as I stepped up on the curb of Madison and 76th. We made our way back to the hotel, and Jack described what he had seen. He said that when Dinah had arrived alone, she sat down in front of the hotel to wait for me, giving the impression that she would stay there until hell froze over if nec-essary until her master came.

Over the next few days, the Lady would not leave my side. Getting frantic even when I just took a shower, she would de-mand to be let in to lie on the bath mat.

This incident was clearly the most frightening of my life with Dinah. While it may have strengthened our commitment, we didn't need the traumatic experience to prove what Dinah and I meant to each other. Infatuation had grown into love long before—somewhere along the road.

BETTY

$\mathcal{L}$ ET'S TAKE TIME OUT for a breather. I would like to move fast forward for a few minutes and talk about three special days during Christmas of 1989, when my friendship with the Sullivans crossed over into a whole new dimension.

For ten years the Sullivans have rented a condo in Winter Park, Colorado, where the whole family (including first Dinah, now Nelson) goes skiing for two weeks at Christmas time.

Each year for the past several they have generously invited me to come for a visit during their stay, but I never quite made it. Finally, they convinced me that an unattached female of uncertain age would not be excess baggage. So with this book as a logical excuse, I joined them in Winter Park for three of the best days in memory.

No, I didn't ski or even attempt to, having promised the *Golden Girls* company I wouldn't jeopardize production. (How's *that* for a classy cop-out?) But the opportunity to spend some round-the-clock time all together was, to put it inadequately, rewarding. Since this was Nelson territory now, Dinah waited for me at home.

This Sullivan family tradition began in 1980. *Good Morning America* had sent Tom to do a story on the Winter Park Sports Center (now known as the National Sports Center) for the Disabled. It was Hal O'Leary, founder of the Center, who gave Tom his first ski lesson. On camera, no less.

None of the Sullivans had ever had any particular interest in skiing, but that changed dramatically when Tom came home and announced, "Now I know where this family is going to spend Christmas from here on!"

Today all the Sullivans are not only good skiers (except Dinah and Nelson) but share a priceless annual family experience. Blythe and Sully each bring along a pal, as a rule, and a couple of the nearby condos are rented by the same returning families each year—all close friends of the Sullivans. It makes for a great and good group.

I arrived in the early afternoon, two days before Christmas, and everyone came tumbling out into the snow to greet me. There were Tom and Patty, Blythe and her friend, Wendy Boyer, Sully with his buddy, Marlin Sheek, and Nelson—who was so completely caught up in the mood of the moment that he kept leaping in and out of snowdrifts like a dolphin at sea.

By the time we all got sorted out and settled, the afternoon began to darken and the clans started to gather. By dinnertime there was a happy assortment of about twenty, ranging in age from an infant to grandparents.

The kitchen was an open area off the living room so, in such close proximity, I thought it would be a great learning experience to see how Patty handled that many people. She even let me help, by handing me a bowl of something and telling me to brush it on some chicken wings that were already in a large flat pan. I did as I was told, then put the pan in the oven, and afterward Patty told everyone I had made the chicken. Well, I didn't want to make a liar of her!

In the meantime, while we were eating "my" chicken wings, Patty turned out a heavenly roast lamb dinner complete with all the other goodies and never missed a beat at the party. Damn! I didn't watch closely enough and learned nothing. As Dinah Shore tells anyone who'll listen, "As a cook, Betty is hopeless, but she does shine at clean-up."

The truth will out, I suppose, so I may as well admit it. I got to sleep with Nelson—and on my first night in town.

When bedtime finally rolled around that first evening, Sully and Marlin weren't back yet, having gone into town earlier to check things out. I asked if it would be okay if Nels bunked in with me, and everybody was too polite to refuse. Happily, I wound up with this big lunk taking his half of the bed out of the middle for the night. He didn't miss a snore all night long, as though sleeping with a major television personality was a run-of-the-mill experience!

For the record, every night thereafter until I left, I noticed the boys made it home before bedtime and my bed partner deserted me.

Next morning, we all rallied early. The boys were all going skiing, but Patty had insisted, over my protestations, to forego the skiing to spend the morning showing me Winter Park.

Blythe and Wendy were going to take all the little girls between the ages of four and about ten (there were several) and give them a ski lesson, Sully and Marlin were off in another direction to challenge a really brutal ski run, and Tom looked ready for anything in a smashing, almost iridescent sapphire-blue ski suit.

Patty also looked terrific, but what else is new? Warm and completely down-to-earth, Patty also happens to be beautiful, with her big blue eyes and ready smile. She always manages to be superbly groomed and dresses up a storm. It's fun to see the genuine joy Tom takes in what she *looks* like as well as what she is. He teases her about being a world-class shopper, but he also knows his wife sees to it that he always looks pretty terrific himself.

It dawned on me that I've taken that fact for granted for years. Tom is always so well turned out—witness this morning's vision in blue—but how is that accomplished? Patty lays his clothes out when he's home, but what about when he's on the road? C'mon, Dinah's good but not that good, nor is Nelson.

Patty explained. "It's a very simple system that works. When I pack for him, each outfit goes on one hanger—suit, a couple of shirts, tie, socks. Tom knows that when he pulls out that hanger, everything goes together. That's how his mom always did it."

Tom grinned at her. "If I ever make my wife *really* mad, she could sure get even."

I love to watch Patty with Tom. She takes obvious pleasure in the fact that Tom is usually the dynamic force in any gathering, although she is always caught up in the general give-and-take. When she helps him with anything—a plate or a glass—it is done unobtrusively. At a restaurant, Patty reads Tom the menu while the others are making their own momentous decisions. And when the order arrives, if it is necessary, she cuts up his serving. It all happens so naturally, no wonder it's often easy to forget that Tom can't see. Always, without interrupting the flow of conversation, there is a quiet "Thank you, Patty" from Tom. Nice not to be taken for granted after twenty-plus years of marriage.

Being in the high country in the snow is therapy in itself, but there were some nifty bonuses. This morning was one. Patty was taking me on a Snocat ride (a tractor with an enclosed cab and a driver) that takes you to the very tops of the various ski runs, up where the highest lifts go. It is absolutely breathtaking, particularly to a non-skier. You can see the world suddenly drop away without having to confront it.

There were skiers of all ages, shapes, sizes, and degrees of expertise on the slopes, including those from the aforementioned National Sports Center for the Disabled. "Disabled" is a misnomer, because giving the regular skiers a run for their money were a number of amputees, several paraplegics on sit-skis—even quadriplegics on tows. Their passion for the sport is contagious and admits no obstacle.

The ride up gave Patty and me some relaxed one-on-one time, normally hard for us to come by with our two busy schedules. We talked of many different things as we rode higher and higher into those beautiful mountains, but mostly we talked about Tom.

Patty knew from the moment she met Tom that he was it for her. There were some hurdles, she freely admits, and it took Tom a little while to realize it, but there was never any doubt in her mind.

It was a good moment to ask her about something I had wondered about on occasion. "Does Tom have a hidden tendency to distrust people's motives sometimes?"

"Yes, down very deep he does. I think it's because, when he was growing up, he couldn't ever depend on people living up to a commitment. Even when he was in boarding school, he'd count all week on going home on the weekend, but sometimes his father just didn't show up. Even today, with his friends, he doesn't rely on promises. But so much of that comes from his childhood."

Eleven years ago, Patty founded an organization called Vistas, which raises money for the Institute for Families of Blind Children. They work with infants and toddlers right from birth, as well as counseling the families.

As she explained, "Working with these little ones and their parents, I began to understand what Tom's mom had gone through. Marie has told us about going places with her blind child, even to the store, and how thoughtless—even cruel—people would be. Today, mothers have much more of a support system. There are new techniques—counseling. They are even allowed a mourning period in the beginning to adjust. Tom's mom had none of that. I don't know how she did it."

Each year the Institute puts on a special fund-raiser, the Tom Sullivan 10K Run. This is the largest one-day charity sporting event in the country, and it has raised well over a million dollars. Far from being one of those "in name only" events, Tom, who has been a serious runner for years, lends his body, as well, and is an active participant in the race.

Training for this run and the other marathons in which Tom takes part is grueling work. Even the invincible Dinah had limits to her endurance, as does Nelson. So it is Patty who runs with Tom most of the time. "Tom has a total lifetime commitment to health and fitness. I had never been into sports before I met him. Now I love it. But although I make a real effort to keep up with him, he is always ahead of me."

The Snocat continued to crawl up the mountain. As we reached the very highest vantage point, standing there, grinning from ear to ear, was one Tom Sullivan. As a surprise, he had planned where to intercept us, and now, looking like the Cheshire Cat, he waved and took off.

There is no way of describing how thrilling it was for me to see Tom ski. As a non-skier I had never dreamed I could get up there to see him. He was easy to track in his electric blue—flying down a difficult run, with his friend John Woodward, acting as his guide, a few feet behind him, and having to ski hard to stay within voice range—then both of them disappearing over the edge of the world. I couldn't believe it! The goose bumps I felt were not from the subzero weather.

Patty and I climbed back into the Snocat. Our trip back down the mountain took a bit longer than Tom's, as it was slightly less direct and nowhere near as spectacular. If Tom and Patty had hoped for a reaction to their surprise, they got it.

One of the clues to Patty's remarkable balance lies in her understanding of her husband's all-out approach to life. Tom has never taken the easy road to anything, and this can, on occasion, lead him into potentially dangerous situations. Only the night before, I had heard about a classic example that had taken place just before the Sullivans left for Winter Park.

Two young men, Mark Wellman and Michael Corbett, had set out to scale the sheer rock face of El Capitan in Yosemite National Park. This is a tough enough challenge for anyone, but Mark was a paraplegic!

Tom Sullivan had been riveted to the TV reports on their progress, and once he learned they had made it safely to the top, he immediately obtained the rights to their story for film and television. Tom and his partner, Jodie Lewis, wasted no time in writing the script, the film to be called "Hand Over Hand."

In true Sullivan form, Tom decided that he didn't want to write about rock climbing without the actual experience, so he persuaded Mike Corbett that they should do a somewhat less formidable climb together.

All went well until Tom got stuck in a crack. He insisted he wasn't in actual peril, because he was belayed on a rope to his partner. The way it is supposed to work, Mark would be able to support Tom on the rope and then let him drop a short distance at a time until he was down. But unable to see, stuck in a crack, Tom was completely disoriented and began to wonder if maybe this time he had bought the farm. "Panic begins to pull at you," he said. That's a lot for Tom to admit.

Well, it had pulled at me too, just hearing about it. And I had marveled at Patty's calm acceptance—as I did again now—having just seen Tom barreling down the slope.

"Patty, how are you able to handle it—seeing him take such chances?"

Her answer came a little slowly. "Of course it scares me. But you see, all his life Tom has had to do that—to try what would seem impossible for him. He's told me how, even as a little boy, he always figured the only way he could be *equal* was to be better. But he's not just being reckless when he does these things; he's sure he can make it, and he won't quit until he does. That's Tom. He must be who he is. How could I ever want to change that—even if I could?"

The Snocat arrived back at our starting point, and there was the conquering hero to greet us, grin still in place, *very* pleased with himself. It was decided that Patty would collect the covey of little girls and take them home while Tom and I got a bite to eat. Then she'd pick us up later. Tom stowed his gear in the car, Patty took off, and we headed for the big cafeteria at the lodge.

After shamelessly overloading our trays, we were lucky enough to find a table by a window overlooking one of the slopes full of skiers. We settled into some serious chowing down, but it would take more than that to shut the two of us up.

Tom was still chortling over how well his surprise had paid off, and I was euphoric after a whole morning spent in that rarefied air and Patty's good company.

"Tom, how did you ever luck in to a girl like that? And she hasn't caught on to you *yet!*"

I expected some smart answer in kind, but Tom surprised me and squared up.

"Along with everything else, she's my best friend. I know that you and Allen had that too—a lot of people don't."

The conversation had suddenly taken on another color. Having just heard Patty on the subject of Tom, I was interested to hear it from his side.

"Sure we don't always agree, but after twenty years there is that central commitment, I guess you'd call it, and we can compromise. That's good, because it's necessary for us to share so much. Patty does the paperwork that goes along with my business, as well as all the family stuff, and we're both very seriously into physical fitness."

"That's putting it rather conservatively," I said.

"But with all this interdependence," Tom continued, "there's always such intimacy. Patty often expects me to be more than I am, but she gives me the never-ending sense that I am the most important person in her life. So many men don't have that, but that's what creates the confidence to try and be all the things she believes I can be. I have come to love Patty more today than I ever thought possible."

I watched the skiers for a moment. Then Tom spoke again.

"For years, I believed Patty wondered if I loved her as much as she loved me. Frankly, she had good reason. I was living my life in the fast lane—show biz, rock and roll. Not the most conducive environment to hold a marriage together."

"But you did."

"Patty did, thank God. But there were rough times. Very rough times. In the early days, as my career was moving along, Patty was responsible for everything. If I had an appointment, she had to make sure I got there, and very often there was tension in the process. I can remember many days when I would have a meeting to attend and Patty would have to load two children and a husband into our small Volkswagen, then sit in somebody's office or in the car during a casting audition, trying to keep the kids under control while I tried to make a living."

For once, I didn't interrupt.

"Dinah changed all that. Her ability to do her job not only gave me more independence, it allowed Patty to become far more relaxed at handling all the tasks that went along with being the mother of two small children and the wife of a demanding blind performer attempting to make it in show business.

"On the other hand, Dinah provided *me* with freedom, too. That meant the ability to come and go as I wished. When I would be working on music—along with my rowdy musician compatriots—I'd often lose track of not only what time it was but what day it was. Although I can say I was always a fiscally responsible husband, I wasn't always an emotionally responsible adult. Dinah provided the freedom that let me spread my wings and fly, sometimes at Patty's expense."

I had never heard Tom speak so openly about those difficult early years. They had only been vaguely alluded to as "the rough times." It threw a new light on a conversation I had had with Patty once about Dinah which had surprised me at the time.

We'd been talking about Cay and Dinah, about how Cay was friendly with Tom but just co-existed with him. Cay was Patty's dog. Patty's assessment of her relationship with Dinah was not quite what I'd expected.

"I've always loved Dinah, of course, but she was definitely Tom's dog. I could feel her resentment when I'd accompany them. Dinah was always sweet with me, but there was no real basic rapport. It was as if there was a line drawn: 'This is as far as it goes.' I almost felt I was infringing. It sounds funny, but as females you and I both know that you don't cross certain boundaries within relationships."

At last I could understand Patty's slight reticence. Dinah's early Sullivan years were not golden ones for Patty. As wise as both those ladies are, there had still been room in their hearts for the green-eyed monster.

Tom pushed back his chair. It was time to go find Patty. As we walked out, he added, "We made it through only because Patty knew what a marriage should be. Today I can't believe how rich our lives are."

We stepped outside into the clear frosty air to find Blythe and Wendy sitting on the veranda ready to ride home with us. Naturally, I couldn't wait to tell them about seeing Tom ski and the Snocat ride. It wasn't long before Patty pulled up and we all piled in for the ride back.

"What blows my mind, Blythe," I said, "is the skier who is *guiding* Tom! I know you've guided for your dad a lot. How in the world did you learn to do it?"

"By watching the clinic-certified instructors all those years, I guess. Sully guided Dad before I did. Sully can also ski as an amputee. That means he skis on one leg, using special poles— they call 'em outriggers. He wears one ski boot and just an après-ski sock on his other foot."

Tom interrupted. "Come on, Blythe. You're the best guide I've got." He put his arm around her. "In fact, it was during my learning process that we began to be pals."

Tom went on to explain that guiding a blind skier is about as difficult as it gets.

"She has to look beyond me and read the course before I get to it, as well as look uphill to make sure it's clear. To call the turns appropriately, she must turn when I turn, or we wind up far apart."

"How close do you stay behind him, Blythe?" I asked.

"Well, if we're on a mountain by ourselves, I let him go ahead but within voice range. When it's crowded, I stay just a step above him. He used to get so mad when we first started. I'd say, 'Okay, okay,' and he'd say, 'I need *words*!' "

Tom cut in. "Yeah. I'd say, 'What the hell does "okay" mean? Gimme "go" or "left" or something.' Sometimes the tips of her skis would actually touch the backs of mine. If I screw up, she can't stop. We're not only down, but somebody's hurt."

"Dad, remember the day I steered us into powder up to our

necks? You kept falling, and every time we'd have to stop and dig into the snow to find your dumb skis."

Tom recalled another day when he and Blythe arm-in-armed all the way from the top of the hill to the bottom. He explained to me that arm-in-arm meant they held hands, never turning, as they rocketed down the mountain. "I can remember yelling, 'Whoa, Blythe. We're going too fast. You're out of the will if you don't slow down!' But she never did."

It felt good to return to the warmth of the condo. The living room was dominated by a beautiful Christmas tree, next to which was a handsome wooden rocker facing the fireplace. There was always a fire burning—not roaring, just quietly there, so that it almost seemed like another living part of the family.

The rocker was Tom's headquarters. It was near the entry stairway so that, sitting there, Tom was aware when anyone new entered the room. From there he was in charge.

When Tom was twenty-six he wrote his first book, *If You Could See What I Hear.* It told the story of his childhood and young life and was subsequently made into a feature film. Very early in the book he speaks of motion:

> In my first two or three years, I was, of course, un-
> aware of the emotional family drama created by my
> blindness. I didn't know what blindness was, simply be-
> cause I did not know the meaning of sight. A swing,
> rusted and squeaking, was the center of my universe. A
> vivid early memory is of the day I discovered that I could
> twist the swing and then, on its unraveling, be spun
> around at speed. Movement, for a blind person, is as im-
> portant as the sweep of eyes for a sighted person. This is
> the reason many blind children, whether they are sitting
> or standing, are almost always rocking, always moving. A
> sighted person is constantly aware of motion—a curtain
> blowing in a breeze, a person walking across a room,

someone shifting papers on a desk. When a blind person moves, he feels he is a participant in the action about him.

That long-ago three-year-old was still there somewhere in the Winter Park living room, for Tom never stopped rocking. He would unconsciously punctuate his conversation with the movement of the chair, and the more intense the discussion, the faster he would rock. A big laugh would really bring him up to speed. All the while, Nelson would lie at the head of the stairs, just far enough from the rocker to be tail-safe.

Nelson. Even if there hadn't been all the other things that made the Winter Park trip so special, it would have been worthwhile simply for the opportunity to observe Nelson off-duty— the family member in his home setting.

I had met Nelson on two occasions at the Sullivans (both times Dinah had stayed home to avoid confusing any priorities) and found him to be a very nice guy. True, he tended to hang out mostly by himself, or at least until Sully came home. From then on, where you found young Tom, you found a big black Labrador.

The next time I had seen him was when Patty and Tom and Nelson came up to Seattle for the annual meetings of the Morris Animal Foundation. Tom had, by now, joined this fine organization as a fellow trustee and active participant—so active, in fact, he later became President of the Foundation.

Seeing Nelson under such different circumstances was a revelation. Replacing the laid-back Sully buddy I'd met at home was this no-nonsense, super-efficient working machine. He led Tom through all the meetings and gatherings of unfamiliar people in strange territory as if he were a charter member of the group.

On this Saturday, Tom was our luncheon guest speaker and we had a capacity crowd. Nelson had snoozed under the table throughout the meal, but when the time came, he led Tom onstage and sat at solemn attention as Tom opened with a song at the piano. When Tom rose and moved to the lectern to speak—and what a wonderful speech it was—Nelson figured to catch a few more zzz's stretching out flat on his side where no one would notice—center stage! Toward the end, as Tom began his closing remarks, Nelson sat up with a yawn as if on cue, ready to galvanize into action again full tilt.

After four days of Morris meetings, we flew home to Los Angeles on the same plane. Tom and Patty were in the first row, Nelson at their feet, and I was directly across the aisle. As the other passengers boarded, I literally had a front-row seat for a funny exchange, when one of the flight attendants leaned across Patty to address Tom.

"Sir, may I help you put your bag in one of the upper bins?" She reached for the sleeping Nelson, a black blob at Tom's feet. Nels lifted his head and the girl jumped a foot.

"Oh, my goodness! I guess not!"

When it happened again a moment later with a different attendant, I really cracked up, but Tom says it's par for the course on almost every trip. Asleep, with his square harness and glossy black coat, Nelson could qualify as a very smart piece of carry-on.

I had come to Winter Park having seen both faces of this fine animal, but I still hadn't been able to reach behind his natural reserve. Admittedly, despite all her virtues, Dinah could be called easy. By contrast, my acquaintance with Nelson was still rather general. His affection and comfortable participation was apparent, yet there was a remoteness about him that was hard to define. I got the distinct impression that this was one very serious dog. He loves to run full out as an athlete, but it is hard to picture him playing with a toy. Try as I would, I couldn't seem to find a sense of humor.

Well, the morning after my arrival, Sully and his pal, Marlin, returned from early skiing and blew the above assessment right out of the water.

To begin with, Nelson always starts vocalizing the minute he lays eyes on the boy, and he keeps up this exclusively-for-Sully language long after the initial greeting is over. There followed a ridiculously giddy game with one of Sully's socks, which Nelson obviously had been anticipating. The object of the game, apparently, was to see which participant could get sillier as they wrestled over the sock prize.

When I said I was surprised to see all of this frivolity in Nelson, Sully said I hadn't seen anything until I'd watched Nelson play with Cay back home.

"They play *all* the time, and Cay always lets Nelson win!"

Big Tom joined in. "Cay used to be Dinah's outlet, too. She'd come home stressed out from a trip, and good ole Cay would be there with his play therapy. Somehow Cay has always been comfortable with the role he chose for himself—low German shepherd on the totem pole."

Tom went on. "In no way does this playboy tendency detract from Cay's early Schutzhund training when it comes to protecting his home and family from the outside world. He seems to know one doesn't have anything to do with the other.

"It was during the time I was on the road so much with *Good Morning America* and we were concerned about Patty's security at home alone that Cay came into the picture. We got him from Germany. His formal name is Cay vom Schlöss Westhusen and he is third-degree Schutzhund, meaning he has been trained to protect his family. Totally.

"For the first three months we had him, Patty took him out to Riverside and worked with a police trainer so she could learn the obedience training that Cay already knew.

"She went through the whole bit—the biting exercise where the dog would attack the trainer who was wearing a glove, and Patty would have to call him off. She'd yell *Plotz!* and Cay would let go and lie down instantly. And the chase—where he'd run a suspect off without ever actually touching him. Thank God we've never had to use any of that, but I feel better knowing it's there for her in an emergency."

Watching Sully and Nelson together, it figured that these two intense teenagers would migrate toward each other.

At seventeen, Sully assumes a tough, macho cool that can sometimes be off-putting to his outgoing father, and it is interesting to see these two deal with each other on occasion. They are true friends and share not only unlimited father-son love but deep respect. However, young Tom Sullivan, Jr., is bursting with all the harnessed energy of his age and the universe, and sometimes wants to do things *his* way. Not unlike the dynamic Nelson. Is it any wonder these two forged the bond that they did, each trying so hard to prove his identity?

Over our relaxed three days together I saw a different side of both of them. I was amazed to discover that under all his "coolth," there was great sensitivity and awareness on Sully's part, and absolute devotion on Nelson's.

Next morning, Patty went skiing, Marlin was still asleep, and Tom and Sully and I found ourselves kicked back in front of the fire. We were having what was tantamount to a great bull session. Nelson, as usual, was sound asleep by his pal.

There are two love seats at right angles to each other in the condo living room, and if Sully was on one, Nelson was automatically at his side; the rest of the world would just have to accommodate. So when Sully invited me to join them, I felt duly honored, even though neither Nelson nor I are really built for three-on-a-love-seat.

Sully is conscious of every breath the big dog takes. At one point Nels was twitching in his sleep, as all dogs do from time to time. Sully interrupted himself to remark on it.

"He's dreaming. He does that sometimes at night on the bed. I don't wake him up, I just hold my hand up to his nose for him to get the familiar, secure scent, and he settles back without even waking up." Sully suited the action to the word, running his hand tenderly over the big black nose. Nels gave one guttural moan of satisfaction, pushed all four legs out (nearly landing me on the floor), and continued his slumber.

When Tom speaks of Nelson, his admiration is boundless. He speaks of the dog's love of the work, attention to the job, super talent—especially on their more recent trips alone together. It is almost like listening to a benevolent employer taking great satisfaction in a fine employee. Maybe that's the way Nelson has sorted it out for himself: Tom as the respected boss, Sully as the deep and forever buddy.

"But obviously Nelson loves you," I said.

Tom shrugged. "Nelson's love is as hard to figure as a teenager's. Does he mean it or does he think I'm a jerk? Maybe Nelson feels my love is conditional. Maybe I'm trying too hard, which can upset both of us."

There was an interesting analogy between these two young males of Tom's. I could remember Tom saying something along those lines to me a while back in California, although in another context, following a disagreement with his son. At that time, the discussion had been about trying to get through to a teenage boy, and Tom had said, "I told Sully I can read voices. I can usually get all the nuances, but I can't read all the shrugs and blinks and body language. When you don't talk to me, I'm lost!"

It was good to be sitting in front of the fire with all parties involved relaxed and tension-free.

As we sipped our coffee, Tom went on rocking and talking about Nelson and Dinah, citing some of the differences in their approach.

"A dog—any dog—knows when I don't know. They can feel uncertainty through the harness. When Dinah sensed I didn't know, she would always question by turning her head. But Nelson is going to get me there anyhow, come hell or high water. He says, 'If the world is flat and not round, I'm walking off the planet. I don't care!' "

It reminded me of some of the early reports I'd had on Nelson from our mutual limo drivers in LA. "Dale told me how he had always been accustomed to watching you come out of the airport with Dinah. He'd see her daintily size up the doorway, then guide you through it. He said it came as something of a shock the first time he saw Nelson's attitude toward that same door—'I'll get him through this sucker!'—and out you came full throttle!"

We all laughed, but Tom went on. "With Dinah I could keep a low profile. Nelson's gung-ho attitude proclaims to the world, 'Here comes a blind man!'

"As far as the quality of their work is concerned, Dinah and Nelson are equally magnificent in what they accomplish. It's really nobody's fault that they *perform* that work so differently."

He chuckled. "I've thought a lot about this. It's like basketball. Nelson is the playground player. He's the kid who can make every jump shot—he can jump to the moon. But when it comes to the game crunch, he may lose it. Let's say he's given four choices. Nelson will make an instant decision and wind up with maybe a fifty-fifty result.

"Dinah, on the other hand, is Magic Johnson. Given the same four alternatives, Dinah will take a split second to think, then make the right choice and go on to win the game."

Once again, at the expense of sounding like Nelson's defense counsel, I felt obliged to point out the considerable age differential in Tom's two-dog equation. Nelson's percentages are improving perceptibly as they spend more time together. Not only was it unfair to compare raw young Nelson to the seasoned Dinah, there was also a vast difference in Dinah's early Tom from the

Tom who works Nelson today. It is almost as if the dogs' roles should have been reversed in time.

Tom conceded the point. "I have to admit, I work differently with Nelson. With Dinah, our communion was consistent. I would read what I figured she was thinking and then verbalize it. I don't do that with Nels."

Tom's use of his black friend's name is not without a significance of its own. When he is speaking casually, or they are in a relaxed situation, it is "Nels" or "Nel" or even "Nelly." However, when they are working or when Tom is addressing the dog seriously, it is always "Nelson." When I remarked on this, Tom said, "It's like with my son, I guess. He's Sully most of the time, but if I'm making a serious point, it's Tom."

He suddenly turned to his son and smiled. "Sully, why do you like Nelson so much?"

Without missing a beat came the answer: "Because he loves me back."

It wasn't quite the answer Tom had expected. There was a moment's silence.

"Don't forget, Dad, when Dinah came I was a little kid and there were lots of people ahead of me with her. But when Nelson came it was kind of love at first sight. We understand each other."

From that morning on, for the rest of my stay, whenever Sully was out, Nelson began to join me on the couch, where he thoroughly enjoyed all the petting and attention—always, however, with his back toward me. But when Sully was there, the big dog would curl *into* him, with his head resting in the crook of Sully's arm. In fact, the night we all opened our Christmas gifts, Sully had to open his over the head of the sleeping mound in his arms.

That evening, Tom and Patty had arranged a night sleigh ride for the whole group into the back woods of the Colorado mountains. It turned out to be something straight out of a Hallmark greeting card.

The night was crystal clear and icy cold—12 degrees below zero. It was too cold to let Nelson run with us, and the two horse-drawn sleighs were filled with Sullivan friends and their families. So Nelson missed a perfect evening.

We were dressed warmly, naturally, but as everyone piled onto the sleighs, the drivers tucked us all in with extra blankets. Warm and cozy, we were driven straight out into the woods for an hour to a rustic log cabin. No electricity existed. The only lighting was candles and kerosene lamps. Yet waiting for us when we arrived was a delicious, very uptown, catered dinner. Don't ask me how they did it—call it Christmas magic.

Predictably, we had all been singing carols for the whole ride out, and at one point Patty said quietly, "Tom, please sing 'O Holy Night.' I love the way you do it."

Very simply Tom began to sing, and in that crisp, thin air his rich baritone seemed to fill the world, accompanied only by the sleigh bells on the horses. Trust me, boys and girls, *that* was a moment.

After dinner, on the way home, we stopped the sleighs and everyone hushed for a minute to listen to the silence. Well, of course, once we paid attention, it wasn't silence at all, but stillness, filled with small sounds: breathing of horses, creak of leather, wind through pines, clumps of snow landing on snow. More Christmas magic.

When we started up again, Tom said, "Tell me what you see. Describe it to me."

One poor insensitive soul piped up with "We can't see anything—it's dark."

Someone else began to describe all the things there were to see; the black pines against snow that seemed to have a light of its own, the navy blue of the sky, the stars, the bobbing heads of the horses. Tom has a way of making everyone see better.

For all the years, it has fascinated me how clearly Tom "sees" things. It isn't as though he had lost his sight at some point along the way; he's been blind since birth, so he has no early mental images to aid him. That doesn't stop him from constantly seeking more and more information for that computer in his head. I remember reading somewhere that we so-called "normal" people get ten times more information through our eyes than through our ears, and yet, time and again, Tom will be aware of something long before anyone else has even noticed. His perception, especially in the evaluation of people, is mind-boggling. Is it really just a matter of making do with the tools you've got?

When I brought this up to Tom, he explained that people with sight cannot look at any*one* or any*thing* for long without losing concentration.

"It's the other way around for me," he said. "My concentration builds when I meet someone; I'm not distracted by movement. I zero in on people and stay with them. If I can sharpen up the receptivity of my four senses, so can anyone with five. People who don't develop all the senses they have are only half alive."

There have been times when I have watched Dinah, and I marvel at all the things she can sort out with her incredible nose. But Dinah's nose is constructed differently from mine. Tom's isn't. He has the same instruments for smelling and tasting and hearing and touching as I, yet he uses them to so much better advantage. He swears it's a matter of paying attention and that he has had years of practice doing just that, whereas I get lazy and let my eyes do most of the work for me.

.   .   .

Tom wrote several scripts for Michael Landon's series *Highway to Heaven*, including a recurring role for himself (no fool, he!). A scene I particularly remember was one in which he and a boy, also blind, were sitting on a high cliff and Tom was describing the sun setting across the sea to the boy. When I asked him how in the world he could write something he had never seen, Tom talked about a pal of his in school long ago, Tom Sly. They spent one summer camping on an island off the Cape Cod coast, and evenings were passed in long discussions about everything and anything.

"Tom Sly was neither a poet nor an artist by standard definition," Tom said, "but he was unconsciously both as he attempted to articulate to me, who had never seen, the beauty of a sunset across a stretch of water, the color of a wild flower, the design of driftwood, or the pattern of a shell."

I wonder if Tom Sly ever saw that episode of *Highway to Heaven*.

On my last afternoon in Winter Park, it began to snow. Nothing serious—a light movie kind of snow that completed the postcard. The kind of snow you simply must walk in.

We all climbed into our gear and, looking like spacemen, took off, Nelson leading the way. Tom had chosen to walk with Patty so Nels was off-leash and ecstatic. Tom calls snow the blind man's fog, because it muffles the sounds he lives by. "Who," he said, "but the blind have taken the time to listen to the fall of snowflakes?"

It is so typical of this individual that he even manages to meet snow on its own terms. Leave it to him to have to learn not just to ski—that wouldn't be enough—but to ski *well*.

Under cover of the general conversation and the crunch of our boots in the snow, I hit Sully with a quick question.

"What do you like best about your dad, Sully?"

There was a short pause, then, "He will say 'I'm sorry' after a quarrel if he was wrong. Other parents don't do that."

Sully glanced up to where Nelson was playing snowplow through the trees.

"Come on, Nelly, let me put your leash on."

"What's he doing?" Tom asked.

"Nothing. I just think it's time to put his leash on."

Blythe and Wendy dropped back to walk beside me. Blythe said, "This is where Dinah almost got in trouble," and she went on to tell about one afternoon when they were walking down this same road and Dinah, like Nelson, was having her own great adventure. It seemed Tom called her, and, as usual, she responded instantly, bounding down the hill to him. At the same moment, a delivery van suddenly appeared, coming down the snowy road. Dinah locked all four brakes and the driver did his best, but neither could stop in time. Fortunately, the driver was a split second ahead of Dinah and she slid into the side of the truck, rather than in front of it. She was a little shaken up, but not hurt.

"I just remembered something about Dinah," Sully said. "Remember the first few years we came up here? We stayed in a different condo. Remember how, when we changed to this one, Dinah still always went to that other one first? Every single year!"

That led Tom to something else. "One of the funniest moments I can ever remember with Dinah was the night we went to the tubing hill!"

Tom explained that the tubing hill is a sheer ramp of ice with side rails to keep you moving in a straight line. "You sit in inner tubes and slide down to the bottom, screaming all the way."

"Dinah had come with us, and when I wasn't paying attention she tried to follow Blythe's tube down the hill. She completely lost her balance, slid on her back, and tubed her way to the bottom on her luxurious butt!"

"Her paws were straight up in the air," Patty added. "When she got to the bottom, she stood up and shook, and then she looked up and saw Sully, and bounded back up to the top of the hill through the deep snow. You'd think she'd had enough, but for the next four times, every time one of the kids would tube down the hill, so would Dinah!"

We decided to extend our walk to a charming German restaurant for a huge dinner, complete with all the holiday trimmings. Sully and Marlin and Nelson led the way, Nelson on his regular leash, not in harness. It was fun to see the raised eyebrows of the other diners, when they saw a couple of teenagers bring their dog into a restaurant, and then watch them figure it out.

The big black dog was a model of decorum, tucking himself under the center of the large round table where—you're ahead of me—the sack hound went to sleep.

So it was that over the course of these three Winter Park days, I was able to spend time with all the Sullivans—as individuals and as a family. I realized big Nelson was the catalyst responsible for bringing Dinah to me, which in turn had shifted my friendship with the Sullivans into a whole new gear.

It is also just possible that Nelson could prove to be an important pipeline of communication between the two Toms as well. The tenderness, the awareness, the consideration Sully manifests in connection with his Labrador friend is not lost on his father. However, without the Nelson conduit, those seemingly out-of-character qualities might be overlooked in the daily give-and-take of growing up together. Nelson too, it seems, has work to do that goes beyond the harness.

·   ·   ·

When I returned home from Winter Park, I told Dinah that her Sullivan family and I had learned more about each other, and grown closer over those three days, than we had in the whole past twenty years. Things would never be quite the same between us again. They'd be better.

ACT THREE

9
TOM

AS I BEGIN TO write about Nelson, I realize that Tom Sullivan, Jr., is as basic to this part of the story as is Nelson, and I must note that through Betty I learned as much about the one as I did about the other.

How much stress I must have placed on my two leading men! When I think of Tom having to grow up under the shadow of a celebrity father who also happens to be someone with a disability, I cannot even imagine what that pressure must feel like. No matter what he does to express his self-image or hope for personal success, his actions are constantly compared to those of his father.

I've tried to explain to Sully that life is not a competition. It is supposed to be the celebration of each and every human being's own individual uniqueness: his or her stamp on the world, not a copy of a stamp left by a parent. Who you are is the most important element in your life, and Sully's mother and I are delighted with who he is.

And then, how about poor Nelson? He came to the Sullivan family having to follow in the paw steps of, as my Irish mother would say, "a saint!" Saint Dinah, who did everything perfectly, who was always just right.

There is no denying it was tough in the beginning. Just thinking about it, I shake my head in amazement that we have come so far from where we started with Nelson.

When Dinah and I came home from that last bleak trip, I was faced with a dilemma. I was coming into the busiest time of my adult life; concerts, speeches, even my daily trips into Los Angeles would continue to require the participation of a working animal. My needs aside, it was time to ease the stress on the golden girl.

For the past few months, Smitty had called from Detroit periodically to see how Dinah was doing. He would remind me each time that eight to ten years of actual work was the average for any guide dog. They began to slow down, and masters needed to begin to consider their retirement.

I always figured I would think about that tomorrow. Well, tomorrow was here.

I knew that if I took too much time thinking about all of the ramifications, I wouldn't make that necessary call to Smitty. So, following a long family discussion, I phoned him at home that evening. He was not surprised by the call.

"Smitty," I said. "It's happened. Dinah can't work anymore." I went on to fill him in on what had transpired.

"You must be feeling awful, Tom. What do you want to do?"

"I know I need another dog, but jeez, Smitty, I can't picture my life without Dinah in it."

"I could never find another Dinah, Tom. That animal doesn't exist. You have to accept the fact that another dog will be just that, another dog, another friend, another work companion. *Somebody else.*"

"Okay, Smitty. Find me something totally opposite, a male, for sure—maybe short-haired."

Smitty said quietly, "Tom, I think I have the right dog. I've had a situation here with a dog who somewhere in the back of my head had your name on it. His name is Nelson. He's a black Lab. He's tough and extremely committed. Do you have any trips coming up when you could stop and meet him?"

"I don't have one, Smitty, but I'll make one. I'll come without Dinah. Can you pick me up at the airport?"

"No problem," he said. "When can you come?"

"How about tomorrow?"

"Okay. I'll pick you up right at the gate."

And so there I was, early in 1987, meeting my friend Harold Smith in Detroit and confronting a change I knew was inevitable but devastating. However, at this time I took it for granted that Dinah would still be living at home with our family.

Smitty and I went to dinner at Joe Muir's Seafood Restaurant, one of my favorites. He began to tell me the incredible saga of Nelson; alias Jordan, after Michael Jordan, the basketball player; alias Brando, after Marlon Brando; alias Frazier, after Joe Frazier, the boxer; and probably some others. You see, Nelson had been down the road and back again in guide dog training.

"Tom, this dog is a hardhead," Smitty said, "but he is one of the most brilliant animals I've ever been involved with. In some ways, he may even be smarter than Dinah, though maybe not as accommodating. He is certainly more aggressive, but I'm not sure about his judgment, and he attacks everything like a runaway downhill skier. It seems to me he's just the dog for you."

I asked Smitty what the hell he was talking about with all those names.

"Well, here's his history. When Nelson finished his training, he was given to a blind guy who had a nine-to-five job in Hibbing, Minnesota. Now, Hibbing is a small town with no real transport system, and most of what they did was country travel, walking to work on a road without a sidewalk and then getting on the only bus that ran in the town that would drop him right at his office. He'd do his job and then come home. That was the extent of what Nelson was asked to do."

"So, what was the matter?" I said.

"The guy wasn't particularly athletic, Tom, and a number of times Nelson took him right off his feet. You see, Nelson does everything like an athlete. He'll work right up to an obstacle and stop on a dime. He turns fast, and you've got to be right on top of things to pick up on his cues. I think that's perfect for you. Anyway, this guy rejected Nelson and brought him back to the school.

"We then sent him out with another guy who tunes pianos for a living. I figured the fact that he needed a dog with imagination would be perfect for Nelson. You see, this guy is always going to different people's homes to do his job, and the dog has to be willing to keep trying all the time."

"Well," I asked, "what happened?"

Smitty laughed. "Nelson sure did keep trying all the time! He yanked this guy up and down steps and simply had too much energy for him."

"Then what?"

"Well, Nelson was sent back to the school. Normally, when a dog washes out twice, we figure that's worth giving him a permanent career change. But in this case I just couldn't do it. Maybe I was thinking of you. I don't know.

"Anyway, I started bringing him home with me at night and doing some creative paperwork to indicate that he had been sent out with a family who owned a Michigan farm, as an animal in career change. Then I'd check him back into the school in a few days under a new name and place him in my string of new dogs, starting him in training all over again."

"How long have you been doing this?" I asked.

Again, he laughed. "Oh, seven or eight months. Nelson is probably the most bored and overtrained animal in the history of the school. See, with black Labs, they all kind of look alike, so I could keep smuggling him in and out."

I couldn't contain myself. "You mean you've been recycling this dog for almost a year, waiting to see how long Dinah would be able to continue the work? You're really something! When can I meet this four-legged cyclone?"

"How about tomorrow morning?" he said.

I couldn't wait for morning to arrive. I didn't want any part of a new dog, but there was something intriguing about meeting an animal that Smitty was so high on and had worked so hard to save for the Leader Dog Program—and, I guess, for me.

The next day, we went back into the kennels to greet Nelson. When Smitty opened Nelson's gate, this animal burst out like he was shot from a cannon and headed straight for a large open container of dog food, from which the kennel man was scooping out bowls to feed all of the animals. Smitty just had time to yell a sharp "no!" before Nelson's nose would have been into somebody else's food.

Immediately, I was confronted by the fact that this animal had, and still does have, his own life agenda. I have learned, subsequently, that Nelson may give people the impression of being totally frenetic, but he always has his own purpose. Our continuing goal is to try to extend the concept that *my* purpose must be his purpose.

We worked for the next two days. That's an understatement. We didn't simply work, we competed for control. Nelson was so anxious to do the job, he threw himself into it with so much gusto, it took me completely by surprise. Where Dinah would come up to a street crossing and then slow, perceptibly, and stop so that my feet were right on the edge of a curb, Nelson would roar up to the curb edge and screech to a halt. Where Dinah, with dignity and care, would suggest that a turn was coming, Nelson would drive into the harness, nearly pulling me off my feet, and choose to physically drag me through a left or right turn. My left arm was throbbing so, from the forward harness pressure he exerted, that it was difficult to read his guiding signals. And he had this annoying habit, because of the way the harness came across his chest, of breathing through his mouth as if he was about to go into cardiac arrest.

Smitty found this funny. "All black Labs are like that, Tom. I don't know why the hell they do that, but they're all the same."

"Great!" I said. "This is just what I need on stage for lectures and performances, a hyperventilating Labrador retriever."

However, I could see Nelson's brilliance. Although his cues were nothing like Dinah's, his recognition of circumstance was unbelievable, and his willingness to keep trying until we got it right was limitless. Objectively, I knew I was dealing with a unique animal, but from a subjective point of view, I didn't want any part of him.

Smitty had gotten permission to accompany me to California to spend a few more days trying to figure out if Tom Sullivan could be the jockey for this runaway canine.

We took Nelson through the same kinds of California drills Dinah had done years before. Where Dinah had been careful on our first adventures, Nelson attacked them. I found that my reactions were slow because I was so used to the golden girl.

And, frankly, my fire to begin again was so low that I might not have been trying hard enough.

But I guess we got through the work pretty well because, once again, we were sitting at Hennessey's Irish Pub, having a beer, and Smitty was saying, "I know you guys are going to be great."

"Listen, Smitty, I don't think I want this dog. I think you ought to take him back."

"Tom, don't be crazy. Nelson is special. I'll bet my career on that. I know he can do the job for you in a very different way than Dinah did it, and I think that difference will help you get through this transition without thinking about Dinah all the time. Hell, you're going to have to be on your toes just to cope with Nelson."

I wonder if Smitty knew how prophetic that statement was, because over the years my battle with this young leading man has carried on apace. Sometimes I win. Sometimes he does, but he is an absolutely incredible worker.

When I said goodbye to Smitty the next morning, he said, "Look. I know I've picked the right dog for you. You need an animal that can think for itself, be imaginative, not quit under stress, and adore the work. I know you two are the right combination."

"I'll try to believe that, Smitty," I said, "and we'll work hard."

But, boy, did we have our work cut out for us. One story says it all about my beginnings with this wacko new friend.

Nelson and I were taking our maiden voyage, headed for New York and a speech I was going to give to AT&T. Nelson is fearless, and the first part of the trip had gone without a hitch; that is, until we arrived at Kennedy, one of America's five busiest airports.

As we got off the airplane and walked down the jetway,

Nelson was perfection: moving through people, diving in and out of the crowd, picking his spots like a broken field runner in the Super Bowl game. This gifted animal moved me quickly and efficiently toward baggage claim—until he was temporarily drawn off course.

There happened to be a little four-year-old boy, sitting quietly with his mother at baggage claim, having a chocolate-chip ice cream. I know it was chocolate-chip because I had to buy him another. You see, in the middle of some of the finest work ever done by a guiding animal, Nelson stopped to have a few licks of the tasty Häagen Dasz special. The child screamed. The mother screamed. I stuttered and stammered my way through an apology, while Nelson, in the true tradition of a very secure work dog, continued to do his job as he saw it— eating the remainder of the ice cream, untroubled by the pandemonium surrounding him.

I have finally come to understand that Nelson *is* brilliant. Nothing avoids his scrutiny, and no animal has ever wanted to do a better job. Nelson is simply hyperactive. After the mellow Leading Lady, I was just not ready for the dark tornado that roared into my life.

Dinah would be a hard act for anybody to follow, but especially so for this overstimulated, overexcited overachiever, and when he joined his new family, I should have seen the Braille writing on the wall from the very first day.

In his first five minutes in our home, Nelson managed to knock a vase off a coffee table, trip Sully in his enthusiasm to get to know him, and then, during his first romp with Cay, the German shepherd, fall into the swimming pool. Even Dinah, for the first time in her life, would not deign to get involved.

And this, I thought to myself, is the creature who is now to become my eyes? May the heavens protect me.

Nelson is also extremely difficult to read. When we're at home, he never seeks affection from me. He always seems to be in a state of constant motion, never stopping in his run through the house or in following Sully, or even in his search for food, for any quiet petting or support from me. It is only when I take him out on the road that I become acutely aware of his sensitivity and his need to be loved. Sometimes before we go to sleep on our king-size bed in some hotel he condescends and licks my face. It's a pretty good feeling.

As so many humans do, Nelson hides his emotions under a rock. He gives the impression of being Mr. Macho, always secure and, as Smitty called him, a stubborn hardhead; that's how I see Nelson and, I must confess, that's also how I dealt with Nelson at first. He was such a powerful animal that I held him to a much tougher discipline than I ever did with Dinah. The more I corrected him, the harder he tried, and the harder he tried, the more frantic his work became. It wasn't until I finally realized that I had to allow Nelson to find his own path to excellence that we came to be great working partners. I finally understood that Nelson desires only one thing—to do the job well. He isn't a dog that can be lured away in the middle of his work in the street by other dogs, or distracted by the patting of a stranger. Today, he is even ice-cream proof.

Once I caught on, we began to grow rapidly as a team. I stopped correcting his mistakes with aggression but, instead, acknowledged his excellence with praise and repeated training efforts.

Does this sound like a treatise on the uniqueness of the man-and-dog relationship? I suppose it does. Doesn't it also apply to man and boy?

So often in my relationship with my son, I would mistake his defensiveness for arrogance rather than hurt feelings. So often, I perceived his lack of participation in school as laziness rather than shyness or concern about failure.

Sully once said to me, "Dad, if I try, I fail, and if I don't try, I fail. So it's better not to try."

Suddenly, I'd had a vivid recollection of an angry young blind boy who had felt just such frustration. I had gone to a school for blind kids, and in that school I was the best at everything I went out for: best athlete, best singer, best student. Then I'd come home on weekends, and I was the kid nobody wanted on the team. And I thought, How do I win? If I'm the best at being blind and the worst at being sighted, how do I win? If only there was some way to explain to Sully that one of the problems for which there is still no cure is the pain of growing up.

It is now my responsibility as a parent, and my responsibility as Nelson's master, to create an environment in which the fear of failure is eclipsed by the desire to try, to go for it. It is my lifetime goal to encourage, in both Sully and Nelson, pride in themselves.

A friend of mine defines pride as Personal Responsibility for Individual Daily Effort. PRIDE. What a wonderful acronym! The problem is that human beings and dogs can take on too much personal responsibility, and fear can make cowards of us all. Both Tom and Nelson had to learn to relax and do their own thing without concern for how I might feel about the result.

Even at this late date, I am certainly anything but perfect in my work with Nelson. According to Smitty, I still make dumb mistakes. One day, Smitty was walking with Nelson and me through a very crowded LAX when all of a sudden somebody behind me yelled, "Hey, Tom!"

Now, I don't know how many faces a sighted person can keep photographs of in the brain, but I have the vocal imprint of thousands and thousands of people I have come in contact with somewhere in my memory bank. For reasons I've never clearly understood, I can meet someone on my travels and three or four years later, meeting the person again, clearly remember the sound of that particular voice. No two voices are exactly alike.

When I heard the "Hey, Tom!" I recognized Martin Mull's voice immediately and turned around to greet him—without giving Nelson any clue as to what I was doing. Once Martin went on his way, after our brief exchange, Smitty gave me hell.

"Do you expect this dog to be a mind-reader, for God's sake? Give him a *signal!*" Smitty tolerates no lapses when it comes to one of his dogs. He wouldn't have let Nelson get away with that mistake. Well, neither could I!

Not just with Smitty but in all guide dog work, a general rule is, "Trust your dog. You are building a bond with the animal. Trust your dog."

The same applies when I think of Sully. Trust your son. Trust that if you rear him effectively and give him the tools to work with, he'll find his own direction in life.

This chapter is not a mea culpa: that is to say, a confession from father to son or master to dog. I have every intention of continuing to be tough on both of them, but I have learned through Betty's writing, and long reflection on my own, that creatures are not necessarily as they seem.

That is not all I have learned from Betty. The great thing about true friendship is that, once it is formed, the bond remains for life. Paths may not cross all the time, but the relationship is one in which it is always possible to pick up where you left off. That's quality friendship, and so it has always been with Betty White Ludden and the Sullivan family.

However, when the Leading Lady brought us together in her special situation, our friendship climbed to another level and Betty became an important member of the Sullivan clan.

One night after dinner in Winter Park, Betty brought up a subject with Blythe and Sully that I was aware had been on her mind for quite some time.

"Just to set the record straight, I'd like you two to know that it wasn't until I read your dad's pages long after the fact, that I knew you weren't in favor of Dinah coming to me in the beginning. So help me, I thought it had been a unanimous decision."

Both Blythe and Sully hastened to make the point that it was not Dinah's going to Betty but parting with her at all that had been the issue.

Blythe was emphatic. "I didn't blame you, I just didn't think Dad needed another dog. Dinah was the best, and no one should follow her."

"Is it any better now that this much time has gone by?" Betty asked.

"Oh, yes." Blythe meant it. "When we came to your house and saw how she was all settled in and happy and everything, but she was still so glad to see us, it really helped. She didn't forget us. The hardest thing was realizing it had been the right thing to do all along. That was hard."

I had always been aware that Blythe had never really warmed up to Nelson. She loved him as a living creature, as she does all animals, but not as an individual. I finally understood why.

Sully had an idea. "Betty, you ought to be our grandmother! You're part of the family!" Blythe agreed, and that is clearly how Patty and I feel.

It must have been the way a little girl felt who knocked on the front door of the condominium in Winter Park. Having heard that Betty was staying with us, she summed up the uniqueness of this woman in a simple question. When we answered the door, she said, "Is the Betty White here?" Not *the* Betty White. Simply, "the Betty White."

Well, if "the Betty White" means a show business institution, I guess she was here. If it means one of a kind, I guess she was. And if it means there will never be another, I guess "the Betty White" certainly was here. As far as the Sullivan family is concerned, she has a run-of-the-play contract.

One of the fascinations about Betty for me is that she is the only true star I have ever known who has a supporting character's personality. That is to say, she has always been an A-Number-One team player. One of the reasons she is so warm to everyone she comes in contact with is that she has never taken herself too seriously. There is no sense of being larger than life or being removed from normal contact for Betty. Her star moves in conjunction with other human beings with ease and style. She is genuinely interested in what other people have to say and what they feel.

Robert Burns, the great Scottish poet, said that mankind spends most of its time thinking behind the beyond. Though to meet Betty, you might feel she is interacting easily, the fact is, she is always abstracting: looking inside things, examining them, processing them in that incredible brain, and storing them for future use. Actually, she could get away with being a blind person if she didn't see.

I know that Betty agonized about taking the Leading Lady into her life. Not because she didn't want Dinah, but because she sensed that there was a grave obligation involved in taking on the responsibility. As it turned out, Betty has played a vital role in the life of this special dog.

Dinah is far healthier today than she was four years ago when she first arrived in Betty's home. Only through this woman's kindness could a dog that had given its life to one master so completely find the possibility of loving commitment to someone else. The environment Betty creates with all her animals has given Dinah a new lease: not just on life but on being valuable—through Betty's friends, who make so much of her; through Betty's public life, which allows Dinah still to go to work; and through the constant love and attention that Betty provides. As Dinah ages, she is living a far more fulfilling life than I would have ever dreamed possible. She is living proof that creatures can become even more valuable with time, if we just give them a chance.

Betty and Dinah have worked out their relationship beautifully, and I can truly say I feel no residual guilt about not being there for the Lady—only pleasure in our continuing love for each other.

Now I intend to spend the rest of my time with Sully and with Nelson, working to be a more understanding dad, compassionate master, and loving friend.

Maybe I haven't blown it yet. Sully and I shared an experience that makes me think that I'm still in the ball game.

The Denver Broncos invited me to go to New Orleans and give a preparatory motivational speech before the 1990 Super Bowl. In the course of the football weekend, Sully and I had the chance not only to be at the team dinner and in the locker room, helping tape legs and give pats on the back, but we rode on the team bus and then spent the game on the sidelines, next to Dan Reeves, the Broncos' coach. We also shared New Orleans, the city of nightlife, music, and good times.

On the flight home I said to Tom, "Boy, Sully, what an incredible time we had."

He looked at me and said, "It sure was." Then, with that ultimate California casualness that belied the bombshell he dropped, he said, "Yeah, Dad. The game was great and Bour-

bon Street was terrific. Being with the ball players was great—
but none of it was as important as being with you."

Fathers and mothers wait for that kind of moment. We hope
our children will give us those pearls, those treasures, those
special gifts that we invest our lives in searching for. Sully and I
have turned the corner. We are father and son in the real, true
awareness of what that means to both of us.

And Nelson? He is still running true to form.

We were in Washington, D.C., not long ago, doing a motivational business film on the subject of adversity, and it was
decided that it would be a marvelous scenic allegory on
achievement if I were to canoe down the Potomac River and attempt to run some small rapids. The director felt it would be a
picturesque touch if Nelson lay in the bottom of the canoe
while my friend Charlie and I moved it through the fast-
running water.

I had spent a day and a half learning to use the paddle, and
although I wasn't expert I was adequate. It was a gorgeous fall
morning in Washington, as the canoe gained speed. Now, Labs
are water dogs. Part of their heritage has been to retrieve ducks
and other water fowl during hunting. But Nelson lived in California where the surf ran high, and, unlike Dinah, this black
Lab had chosen not to swim. So it had never crossed my mind
that he might love the river.

My mistake. A large Canadian goose came in for a landing,
flaps down, directly in front of our canoe. That was all my retriever friend needed. All his instincts kicked in. He leaped
from the canoe, and the next thing I knew, canoe, myself,
Charlie, and Nelson were sweeping away down the river in
fifty-eight-degree water, trying to find some rock or outcropping to hold onto. Thank God, it all worked out. We
clambered from the river, shivering, but true to the traditions

of show business we changed our clothes and went on with the day's shooting.

Toward sunset, the film company informed me that they wanted to get some still photos for the brochure cover and asked if I would sit on a rock, out in the Potomac, while Eric Wold, the young man who has also taken pictures for this book, shot some of the pastoral stills that corporations seem to want in contrast to their hectic work process.

Nelson was very concerned about the fact that I was out on the rock while he was on the shore. So, Eric, trying to be helpful, allowed him to stand on the adjoining rock where Eric was taking pictures. Everything seemed to be going well until I heard a sound that sent shivers down my spine: the squawk of another Canadian goose coming in to land just in front of Eric's rock. The next thing I knew, Eric, Nelson, cameras, and film found their way into the Potomac. The funniest line of all came from the director. No one said, "Eric, are you all right?" or "Someone pull Eric out." The line was "Save the film. Save the film!" And what was the black Labrador's reaction? As far as Nelson was concerned, he was doing exactly the right thing. The water was where he belonged. It was on his agenda.

10

BETTY

A S CO-STAR TO TOM SULLIVAN, Dinah's career in show business was varied and colorful, to say the least.

The theatrical language that Tom and I fell into using in these pages came from the title, although Leading Lady referred to Dinah's work life. But the terms may be appropriate after all.

One of an actor's most vital assets is concentration; and whenever it slips, the performance is diminished. The same may be said of Tom and Dinah. The only times they ever got into trouble was when their mutual focus was momentarily interrupted.

Something else. An actor who is able to continue working in some capacity remains a viable individual. As long as true performers can ply their trade, they will somehow manage to muster the vitality that put them in such a volatile business in the first place. So the analogy works in either context. It is the staying in harness that's important.

So that her transition to my house wouldn't seem too mundane, I would take Dinah to the studio with me sometimes if it was going to be a short day.

First things first: she had to meet the other Golden Girls, who had been hearing so much about her. Bea Arthur and Rue Mc-Clanahan and Estelle Getty were enchanted, of course, and couldn't get over her beautiful manners. They still send messages home to Dinah regularly.

These days, I am happily committed to the NBC television network with *The Golden Girls,* but I have been around since the Stone Age of TV, so I've worked at all three networks at different times. Years ago, I did a series at ABC: *A Date with the Angels.* It is always fun to go back on the ABC lot for a game show or a talk show, as I'm sure to run into many old friends on the crew, and their warm greetings make me feel great. Or at least that's how it was.

One day, shortly after Dinah had joined our household, I was booked for an interview on *Good Morning America.* It was to be done live from California, and the segment would be fed into that day's program emanating from New York. With the three-hour time difference, this meant arriving at the studio in the wee small hours. I got the bright idea that it would be nice to take Dinah on with me, and it would certainly make the interview a heck of a lot more interesting.

The Lady was all for it. She entered the studio like an old fire horse who's heard the bell. This time there was no "Hi, Betty," "Hey, Betty, good to see you." It was "Hey, Dinah, where you been?" "You look *great,* Dinah!" And the hugs were all for one ecstatic golden retriever.

Once we were in our places for the interview, there was the routine picture check from New York to make sure everything was A-okay before we went on the air. Well, the minute the camera came up on us, the messages started feeding in from the New York studio. "Is that *Dinah?*" "Where's Tom, Dinah?" "Dinah, girl, how *are* you?" Need I tell you, when we went on the air, it was Dinah's interview? And she hadn't even spent all that time in the makeup chair!

ABC is by no means the Lady's only network. I produced a game show pilot for NBC, hosted by Carol Channing with John Ritter, Gary Marshall, and Betty White on the panel. It was an old property of Allen's called *Look Who's Talking*—long before, and no relation to, the movie of the same name. We all had a great time trying to match famous quotes with who said them. The set was made to look like a playroom, with a fireplace and lamps and couches, purposely designed not to look anything like a game show. To make it even more homey and less gamey, so to speak, ours was the first show of that genre to have a resident dog. The part was written for—who else?—the Leading Lady. There was no performance involved. All she had to do was make herself comfortable in front of the fire and look reasonably interested and beautiful. It was typecasting. She was even color-coordinated.

Unfortunately, the show was not picked up, but it went well, and I was pleased with the effort. We all had a ball putting it together, Dinah included, and I learned a lot.

One thing I learned was that having a dog on the show was the best idea of all. Dinah's very presence was subliminal therapy for everyone on the set. One of the fellows on the crew put it best. He said, "We do so many of these pilot shows, and everybody is so uptight as a rule, because it is all unfamiliar stuff, and somebody usually winds up yelling at somebody. But Dinah made us all feel as relaxed as she was."

That kind of talk, of course, was music to my ears. I was *so* proud of her. She stuck with me all day, for two long days at the studio, while I was wearing my two hats as producer and performer. With no leash, she would just pad quietly after me wherever I'd go, making friends as she went. I don't usually troupe my dogs, but I'm so glad I did in this case.

The NBC Burbank lot is all cement except for one little five-by-ten-foot planted area outside the Johnny Carson offices. We had received permission ahead of time for Dinah to use that space when needed. A couple of times during the day we would walk out there. I'd say "Park, Dinah," and she'd crawl under the railing, hit the dirt between the bushes, and be back at my side in less time than it takes to write it. What a pleasure she is! I wish I could say my timing was that infrequent during those two days, but I was nervous.

To give each network equal time, I must add that Dinah's territory also includes CBS, since she appeared twice on *The Pat Sajak Show.* The first time, Pat had surprised me. He had set it up with my secretary, Gail Clark, so that Dinah, whom I thought I had left at home, walked out to me in the middle of the interview and settled at my feet, as though born to the grease paint. Rin Tin Tin came on later in the show. It would be nice to report that something magical happened between them, but they completely ignored each other.

Dinah's manners, as usual, were faultless, so much so that a few weeks later, when Tom Sullivan was booked on the show, Pat invited Dinah and me to pull a similar surprise. Once Tom and I were seated on the panel talking to Pat on camera, Dinah was smuggled backstage to Patty, who kept her behind the curtain waiting for the cue. Tom was in the middle of telling the story of Dinah's reaction to Nelson, when out burst the Lady herself, straight into his arms. Tom couldn't see her coming, but he recognized the sound of those feet, long before she reached him.

Patty told us afterward that the minute Dinah had heard Tom's voice she had started doing her camel dance, and it was all Patty could do to hold her until the right moment.

Pat Sajak announced that there had been talk of a spin-off, but unfortunately a *Dinah!* show had already been done.

As luck would have it, Smitty and his new bride, Cindy, happened to be watching the show that night in Detroit, and they called the next day to give a glowing report. Smitty said, "When I saw little Dinah on TV, it brought tears to my eyes."

After I hung up the phone, I knelt down on the floor where she was lying and told the Lady all about it. Especially the part where Smitty had called her "little Dinah."

On another occasion, I had alerted the Sullivans to catch Dinah on the *Tonight* show with me. Tom said afterward that Sully had cracked him up when he said, "Dad, Dinah does more television now that she lives with Betty than she did when she was with you. I guess you were holding her back. She's a big star now!"

Dinah might argue the point. She was *always* a star.

Tom has not only learned to live with blindness, he has turned it around and actually made it work for him. By no stretch of the imagination could it ever be considered a blessing, but his constant reach to compensate has resulted in accomplishments he otherwise might never have attempted.

Every now and then something totally insignificant will bring home to me the degree to which Tom's brain has to work overtime. Like the day he laughed at me for jotting down something I didn't want to forget to do.

"You sighted people are always making notes!"

For the first time I got the picture of how much Tom has to commit to memory.

Even in the course of writing this book, I was so busy with my end that it never occurred to me to wonder what Tom's writing routine was. I write first in longhand and then type it. Not until I received some pages wherein Tom referred to sitting "with my tape machine" did I think about it. I can refer back in the text at any moment, if I wish to rewrite or rearrange, just by flipping a few pages. For Tom, it means he has to ask Patty or someone to read it to him, and from then on he has to keep it in his head.

While far from easy, that's a piece of cake compared to appearing in a scripted television show, which Tom does a lot. To give you an idea of what is involved, let's use *The Golden Girls* as an example. Each show is put together in a five-day week. Monday morning, we all read through the script for the first time and then begin to get it on its feet and block the moves. Tuesday and Wednesday, we rehearse. Then, at the end of each day, we do a rough run-through for the writers and producers. Thursday is camera-blocking day, at the end of which is a full dress rehearsal in wardrobe. Friday is show day. We run through all the scenes a couple of times, go to makeup and hair, then tape the show twice in front of two different live audiences. There is a short dinner break between shows, during which we get notes.

From the first read-through on Monday, the writers continue to hone and polish the material, resulting in a daily flow of new pages with revisions. Since the words are constantly being reworked, we carry our scripts for the first few days, rather than lock in dialogue that is going to change. We all think learning these new pages is somewhat difficult. Silly us!

Tom has to memorize everything from the word go before he can participate even in that initial read-through. Each time there is a change, he has to clear the mental computer to commit to the new material. If the constant learning, unlearning, and relearning is hard for those of us who can see, I can't begin to imagine what a nightmare it must be for Tom, yet he does it all the time. His memory literally works as his fifth sense and it has no down time, except when he's asleep. Perhaps not even then.

Memorizing is full-time for Tom, not just work-related. The Sullivans have recently completed building a lovely new home on a hillside overlooking the sea. Tom kids his wife by calling it "Patty's Palace," and it is true that most of the visual choices, especially the decorating choices, have been hers for obvious reasons. The end result is beautiful.

The new house is less than a mile from their previous home, and while that helped simplify the move, it still meant a complete reorientation for Tom. He had to learn a whole new pattern and memorize a new floor plan, which is on several different levels, to add to the challenge. Where in the other house there had been a step down into a room or a step up into a hall in one or two places, the new house has two steps, or sometimes three or four or more, between levels, plus a flight of eleven brick steps curving up to the front door.

For the first couple of weeks after they moved in, Tom could make me laugh in spite of myself, telling me how he had really "fallen" for the house.

"I fall here. I fall there. I fall down a lot. It's okay if I concentrate on what I'm doing, but if I let my mind wander and switch to automatic pilot, I fall up or down some more steps!" I suspect, at the time, his description of the steps may have been a bit more Anglo-Saxon. However, it wasn't long before Tom had locked in the new floor plan, and he now moves effortlessly from level to level. Or, let's say, he makes it *appear* effortless. The Sullivan trade secret.

Perhaps someday I'll stop being amazed that after all these years, Tom can still amaze me. I doubt it.

For many years, I have served on the Board of the Greater Los Angeles Zoo Association, and Tom had always shown great interest in the subject. One day it occurred to me to ask him if he would like to come out to the zoo with me sometime. When I suggested a backstage hands-on tour, I thought he would crawl through the phone.

"WHEN!?"

A few days later, my friends at the zoo set up just such a tour for us, and I had the chance to watch as Tom touched animals he had only read about.

We started with the birds. A keeper put a small species of cockatoo on Tom's wrist, and the little fellow marched up and down Tom's arm.

"I held a parakeet once, a long time ago, but this guy is so much bigger!"

When a scarlet macaw stepped onto his arm, Tom couldn't believe how heavy it was—and how beautiful. Although he couldn't see the brilliant reds and yellows and blues of the big parrot's plumage, he heard the taffeta rustle of the feathers.

Holding the macaw, Tom said, "The cockatoo was like a high-wire performer. I could feel him put one foot in front of the other on my arm—he'd take two steps, then push off—and he balanced on the points of his toes. But this guy is altogether different. He stands on the center of his feet, like a baseball player digging in. When I was doing the aerial work for *Circus of the Stars,* I was taught to keep my arms wide for balance. Look at this!" Sure enough, the macaw held his wings slightly away from his body for the same reason. (Yes, Tom did a stationary bar act on *Circus of the Stars* with Mary Ann Mobley. High—repeat, *high*—above the center ring!)

Next, Tom met Leadbottom, a vulture that walks like a man and who is the undisputed clown of all the birds at the zoo. He stands three feet tall. Tom described him so accurately I was ready to accuse him of faking his blindness.

"I can't get over his head. It's all bare with just this little down on it. And listen to how his feathers rattle when he moves."

Leadbottom chose that moment to join in the conversation with his guttural "humph!" Very deep.

"It sounds like he's having a gastric attack after too much dinner. And I love the way he walks on his toes and leans forward over the front of his feet like he was round-shouldered."

"Tom," I cut in, "how in hell do you know he walks leaning forward?"

"Because he shuffles. His toe hits the ground first, and he shuffles. He reminds me of a little old man I met in Ireland who managed cemetery plots in the village of Dingle. *He* walked like that."

Tom held Sally, the red fox, and she let him check out her big radar-scope ears and bushy tail.

There is a rare phenomenon of communication that happens between animals and the blind on occasion. I've seen it before. An animal will sometimes put up with handling by a blind person that it wouldn't normally tolerate. Is it in the sensitivity of the touch? I wish Sally could tell me.

We moved on to two of my favorites: our red lemurs, Emmett and Kelly. People-oriented to the extreme, both of these beautiful animals gave us their usual boisterous welcome as we stepped into their cage, jumping on whatever part of us was handy and wrapping their arms around us to hang on. This will get your attention even if you are able to see, particularly since they are each about the size of a healthy cocker spaniel.

Tom's delight was contagious. Emmett didn't leap or jump or push off—he just left his arm around Tom's neck and floated around him. Tom's voice was muffled by the red fur that engulfed him.

"It's like a woman in a fur coat sneaking up behind you at a party! But these animals come from a tropical climate. Madagascar. I would expect bare skin, not this incredible thick fur!"

Tom's apt descriptions fascinated me.

"His nose is small and pointed like my first Teddy bear, and he breathes in and out without opening his mouth. Even his fingers are furry—like a kid who pulls his sweater all the way down over his hands. This tail is what gets me; it's longer than the whole rest of his body. But he doesn't *do* anything with it—well, maybe balance. But what a waste. It should be prehensile!"

Perhaps the highlight of the day for my friend was stepping into the cage with Phoenix, a young adult male mountain lion. Tom had some idea of a house cat, but he admitted he had no concept whatever of what the big cats would be like.

For safety's sake, Julie, the keeper, had put Phoenix on a collar and leash for the occasion. Tom was very quiet as he ran his hands over the tawny neck and back. For his part, Phoenix was purring like an outboard motor.

"He doesn't feel anything like I expected. His fur is like Nelson's, maybe a little more grainy, and it's laid over muscles I can feel. They really ripple! His neck is like a Great Dane's. It doesn't make sense that a cat would have a neck like this and then this little head. It's all out of proportion. And his ears stand straight; they don't droop over like Dinah's!"

When Tom finally left the cage, he stood a moment just shaking his head.

"I'll never forget that."

"Were you scared?" I asked.

"Well, my first reaction when I stepped into the cage was 'What the hell am I doing in here?' I heard this purr, and it sounded like a growl for a second. Then I heard the sound of a chain and realized he was on a leash. Then I forgot about everything but touching him."

As our big finish, we went up to the nursery to meet Mookie, our special treasure—a one-and-a-half-year-old chimpanzee, still an infant in chimpanzee terms. The little one stared back in wide-eyed wonder as Tom explored the tiny ears and fingers and toes. It was a mutual fascination society.

"His hands are so smooth and his thumb feels like it's triple-jointed." Tom went on: "His ears are wide and straight out from his head, and they have a double layer of skin with little hairs between. I can almost get my fingers between the layers."

.   .   .

Tom continues to amaze me. In spite of all the time I have spent in so many different zoos, in so many different places, what a wealth of detail I have overlooked, or simply taken for granted! Rest assured, I shall pay closer attention next time.

Tom's perception is not certainly limited by the boundaries of the zoo. The zoo experience was just one more graphic example of the incredible process of translation that takes place in Tom's brain. Is what he says true—that we all have the same capability but we just don't make full use of it? And is it possible that whatever mechanism is at work for Tom is a similar, tremendously more complex version of what is going on in Dinah's head—enabling her, without language, to translate what we ask of her into appropriate action?

Dinah.

While I was busy asking all those unanswerable questions, I suddenly realized there was one obvious question that *hadn't* been asked. Here Tom was able to describe all the exotic animals so accurately, and yet it had never occurred to me to ask how he perceived the Lady herself, not what she does but what she is.

That was only one of the things I had never asked Tom, in spite of all the time we have spent together. And the more I am around him, the more curious I become.

Perhaps the time had come to address that curiosity. Perhaps it was finally time to do a chapter together.

11

TOGETHER

T OM AND I DECIDED to make a day of it, and we picked a
good one. It was clear and warm. Eric dropped Tom off at
my house and would be back to pick him up late that afternoon.

Armed with a pot of coffee and some coffee cake, we settled
out in the garden on two lounge chairs, sharing a table between us.

Timmy and Cricket lost no time in finding their usual places,
tucked into me; Dinah was at Tom's side under his hand; T.K.
was observing from the house, perched on her shelf in an upstairs window.

Once planted, Tom stretched back in his chair and said,
"Well—we're in your ball park. Where do you want to start?"

"Don't we have to start with Dinah, Tom? You two are so
close it may not be easy to describe her, but will you try?"

Tom thought for a moment.

"Betty, to describe Dinah, I would have to start with my sense that Dinah is utter softness. Everything about her, physically, speaks to that sense. Even when she was young, when I would wrap my arms around her and hug her, she was sheer comfort. It was like entering a large pile of leaves in the fall when you were a kid, or a warm bath, or sleeping under Grandma's down comforter.

"I remember nights on the road when we would check into a hotel and the pillow was foam rubber. I can't sleep on foam rubber, so I used to invite Dinah to share the bed, and then I would sleep at an angle so I could use her as the softest pillow anybody could find. I think we both liked that."

Tom smiled and reached to pat the sleeping Dinah. He didn't have to reach far. He stroked the side of her muzzle.

"This face must be the softest thing in the world, isn't it? It's like the velvet on the inside of a jewelry box. And—I don't know why this is—her ears remind me of old, worn-in slippers; they flop and bend in all directions. I could always tell if she was stressed or thinking about something by feeling these muscles and tendons just behind her ear tense up. The same thing applies to her eyebrows. You watch—whenever Dinah is concentrating very hard on something, she tilts her head slightly to the left, and I could feel her crinkle her eyebrows— the muscles at the bridge of her nose, here, would tighten.

"You know, Betty, I've often wondered about how much the Lady understands about who she is. Does she understand she's a guide dog? I think so, because I believe she understands that I am blind. If we were ever out of town and Dinah and I were in a strange hotel room—say, I was sitting in a chair and then stood up to move across the room—Dinah would move instantly, avoiding the possibility of my stepping on her. But when we were in our own home and Dinah believed I knew where she was—that is, when she was lying in a familiar spot—she treated me like anybody else and didn't move. If I stepped on her, she considered it an invasion of her privacy and would be quite put out!"

At this point, Tim and Crick heard the gardener next door and went flying off to voice their disapproval. The Lady lifted her head, assessed the situation, and made her judgment call: it was not worth her while. She would rather slap Tom's leg with her big foot for more attention. Tom caught the foot.

"These calluses on her elbows are like a man gets who has worked hard all his life; they got thicker and thicker. But now that she doesn't have to work and lie on all those hard surfaces, her calluses are softer!

"Hey, girl! This is a pretty cushy life around here, huh?"

It was a delight, watching their appreciation of each other.

"Her breathing patterns always told me a lot," Tom went on. "When she'd tilt her head up and look directly at me and her breathing sounded shallow, I knew she had to go out and relieve herself. And whenever she was in doubt about what I wanted her to do, she'd almost stop breathing altogether, as if she were holding her breath, trying to make the right decision; there was no panting sound. Then there was what I called her hard rhythmic breathing, when she was totally focused on her job; her head would be extended in a line, her tail flaring out behind her, as she moved straight ahead."

"I still see some of that now," I agreed, "when we take our walk around the block—especially on the downhill side. You describe her well, Tom. All you miss is that glorious color."

We were quiet for a minute. I thought about a world without color. Some people are born with perfect pitch; some with a gourmet palate that can identify ingredients; for some reason, no credit to me, I've always had a pretty fair eye for the subtleties of color. I can often pick a good match without a sample to go by. As a result I respond to color, not only in enjoyment but in mood.

I mentioned this to Tom and his answer was unexpected.

"Color has absolutely no meaning to me. It's just a word, another abstract.

"I'll tell you something else I don't care much about—a rainbow. I know it meant a lot to Dorothy in *The Wizard of Oz,* and I do love the Judy Garland song. I guess I picture a rainbow like dropping a glass bottle and listening to the different pieces tinkle.

"When people ask me to describe what it is like being blind, their perception, as a rule, is that I must just see black. That's because when a sighted person closes his eyes, black is still a remaining piece of information imprinted on the brain. I have no imprinted material. My eyes are nonfunctional. The truth is, I don't know what the hell black is!"

Tom's real eyes had been replaced because of an infection that developed when he was a child. Knowing his eyes are glass, I have never been able to understand how they move so naturally.

"Do they ask you that often, Tom, what it is like being blind?"

"That's usually the thing people want to know. As far as I'm concerned, I see myself as a person who happens to be blind, rather than as a blind person. Blindness is only one of the criteria for measurement, and for me it's way down the list of priorities, behind husband, father, athlete, singer, and almost anything else I can think of. It is other people, who impose their sense of what it would be like if *they* became blind, who make it seem complicated and momentous.

"Don't get me wrong—I would love to be able to see, God knows—but my entire life experience has been molded around the constant that I am blind. Those people who lose their sight somewhere along the way have a far tougher time. *That* concept of adjustment is staggering to me—absolutely frightening! My blindness has forced me to develop unlimited sensory awareness, and everything I learn to sense is a *gain*. If I had once been sighted, I would only think of those things as something less than what I once had!" In his intensity, Tom made the springy patio chair behave almost like a rocker.

"So it's because you grew up having to concentrate on your other four senses that they are so incredible now. Is that what you're saying?"

"They're only incredible to *you*. Sighted people have the option to do the same things. The choices are limitless if you'll only take them. Take sound, for instance—break it down."

Tom and I had discussed this subject. "Instead of just complaining about all the noise that drives me nuts, I should try and see how many sounds I can separate and identify, right?"

Tom grinned. "It's a start. But the senses are so interwoven, it's hard to isolate them. Like taste and smell, for instance—sometimes you can't tell where one starts and the other leaves off. The same goes for hearing and touch. When I meet somebody, I can tell a lot about him just by the way he shakes hands, but at the same time I'm hearing his voice, which is also a dead giveaway as to his self-image."

"No wonder you're so good at evaluating people you meet." I meant it; he was. I had seen evidence of it time and time again.

"Don't forget," Tom said, "none of this is infallible. You only remember when it works! There are other things that help you size up someone. Like body language."

"How can you possibly tell body language?"

"It is amazing how you guys who see underestimate what I am learning about you through your body language. It is easy to tell when somebody is looking at me; their voice is focused right on my face and I feel I am holding them in conversation. Obviously, I can tell when people are slouching or bored: they lean back, or slump in their chairs, and their voices come to me from farther away."

I checked to make sure I was sitting up straight.

"There are all sorts of ways to pick up people's nervousness—

they keep tapping a hand on a table, or maybe their speech pattern sounds rushed and pressed, or their palms were moist when they shook hands, or sometimes there is even a telltale body odor. I can often sense that people are looking all over the place, rather than at me, and I'll tell you something—their discomfort about my blindness gives me a tremendous advantage."

What I was enjoying most about this morning's conversation was Tom's willing participation. I knew that each time I pressed the button on a subject, he would take off on it and I would learn something more about my friend.

I said, "You can be sure I'm going to watch my step around you from here on."

Tom looked smug. "I have some interesting keys to go by. Mostly about women, I admit. Tall ladies, with exceptionally fine legs, always sit in chairs slowly and cross those legs languidly. Voluptuous women are usually round-shouldered, because when they were in the seventh grade they were over-conscious of having large breasts. Ladies with long hair are always shaking their heads. I have no firm research to prove this, but blondes tend to have higher speaking voices than darker types."

I couldn't quite buy this last point and said so. "That's a tough call, Tom. She may not really be a blonde!" Believe me, I knew whereof I spoke.

"The point is, even if I don't know exactly what people look like, I do draw my own sensory pictures."

Tom suddenly switched subjects in midstream, and it was up to me to stay aboard.

"Drawing! Now that's something I have no idea of at all. That a person can draw a picture of something which feels flat and one-dimensional to me, and, through perspective, can imply three dimensions to other sighted people, is totally beyond my comprehension. I really regret the fact that I'll never be able to appreciate great art—Michelangelo or Picasso. I've never understood the concept of art."

I chimed in. "I've never been able to understand what a *camera* can do." We had been sorting through pictures for this book a few days before, so the subject was fresh in my mind.

Tom agreed. "Hell, forget Picasso. I'm in a business that relies on film, and I can't understand a photograph. The idea that there is film speed and lens size and aperture and light meters makes no sense to me whatsoever."

"Join the club!"

"Sometimes it's like I live in a cocoon."

I looked at Tom sharply. It was so seldom I ever heard a note of regret in his voice.

Old "Body Language" Sullivan picked up on my surprise immediately.

"Hey, Betty. Look, I'm not disappointed about things I don't know. You see, that's something basic you have to understand. I was born blind. I have only a scientific curiosity about the world I don't know. I've learned to live with it—or, rather, without it—and the world I live in is just fine, thank you."

It was my turn to read voices. Did I detect a hint of defensiveness? I broke the silence after a moment.

"Tom, if I ask you something, will you give me a straight answer?"

"Of course." His smile was back.

"Does all this talk about your blindness, all the questions—does it bother you? I know I've asked you before, but I just want to be sure you don't resent some of this."

Tom's answer was immediate and rang true. "Absolutely not. On the contrary, I'm enjoying it. You're forcing me to examine some areas I have never really thought about. Let's charge ahead."

By this time, the coffee cake was long since history and we figured it was time for a recess. Perhaps we might even break

out some sandwiches to keep body and soul together. A breeze
had sprung up, and we decided to have our moveable feast in-
doors.

As I fixed a couple of trays and rounded up some iced tea,
Tom leaned against the sink.

"You keep mentioning things I do that I've always more or
less taken for granted. I better be careful that I don't start to
think about it, or maybe it won't work anymore. Like those
cartoon characters who run straight off the edge of a cliff:
they're fine in midair, until they look down and see where they
are—and then they plummet right into the ground. *Splat!*
Maybe I'd better quit while I'm ahead."

I liked the cartoon analogy. "Quit!? I'm amazed. I didn't
think the 'Q' word was even in your vocabulary." I took the
trays into the living room, went back for the tea and Tom, and
we relaxed into our accustomed places. The dogs all ambled in
with us, but everybody knew that begging was out of bounds;
they were content just listening to us chatting and chomping.

"Kids are the ones who can nail you with questions," Tom
said. "I had an experience with a four-year-old who came to
visit us from Texas one time. Little Jason Thomas. As children
often do, he kept studying my face—he was fascinated. As far
as he was concerned, there was certainly something different
about his new friend, Tom Sullivan. Finally, in a drawl you
could cut with a knife, he said, 'Mr. Sullivan, what's the matter
with your eyes?' I told him, 'Well, Jason, they don't work.'
That only stopped him for a minute. Then he said, 'Oh. Want
me to wind them up?'

"When I was working on *Highway to Heaven* with Mike
Landon, there was another boy who thought we could fix my
eyes if we just put batteries in 'em!"

I had a Michael Landon story of my own regarding Tom
Sullivan. "When I saw Mike at the NBC Affiliates dinner, he
told me about another time when you were doing his show, and

toward the end of the week one of the kid actors asked you how long you'd been blind. When you told him you were born blind, Mike said the boy looked at you for a lo-o-ong beat, and then said, 'No wonder you're so good at it.' Do you remember that? It still cracks me up. And you should have heard Mike telling it. You know that silly giggle of his."

As I poured us some more tea, I brought up something else that had occurred to me the night before.

"Sometimes, when I have trouble falling asleep, I'll go through memories in my head. It's like turning pages in a photo album. No plot, just pictures. It dawned on me, Tom, that you can't do that. *Your* memories are all plot and dialogue with no pictures—like radio. What about dreams? Do you dream?"

Tom nodded, almost before I'd finished the question. "I'm often asked that. I love my dreams. Where sighted people dream in visuals, my dreams are very conversational, and they always have a plot. They're very structured—kind of like a late-night soap opera, with all my fears and fantasies as leading characters. Not a bad way to go, huh?"

"What about nightmares?"

"Oh, yes! For years, growing up, I had the same horrible dream over and over again. The main character—I haven't thought about this in a long time—the main character was a *boiler*! His name was Ole and he had a thick Swedish accent."

It wasn't easy, but I kept my mouth shut.

"I suppose it came from the fact that we had a furnace in our house that made a lot of noise, but this boiler would chase me and I was always scared to death."

Leave it to Tom not to have your run-of-the-mill nightmare!

Tom remembered something else. "One day I was in the Beverly Hills Hotel lobby with Heidi—this is for real, this isn't a dream—and a woman came over to ask me about the dog. We chatted for a few minutes, and there was no mistaking that voice. It was Doris Day! From then on, she played the lead in all my dreams—particularly the sensual ones!"

This seemed as good a time as any to clear the dishes away. Tom would probably welcome a few minutes with Doris.

As I came back in to sit down, I brought up a major puzzlement.

"Here's one I simply can't figure out, Tom. You're hung up on all sports, but how can you follow them? How do you perceive them?"

Tom's face lit up. Now we were in his territory.

"I played basketball as a kid, where we'd hook a buzzer on a basket, enough to be able to follow the game. Today, when I hear that Michael Jordan stuffed it, or jammed it, I know exactly what that means.

"Football? I've played enough to understand the concept, and I can throw a football quite well. And I've been on the sidelines where I can hear the blocking and tackling. I can hear the signals. I can hear the ball hit a shoulder pad, so I know the ball was thrown."

Tom rocked faster in his enthusiasm. "I knew I was a sports nut when I started watching tennis. I took tennis lessons for three weeks so I could make the serve. I couldn't do anything after that, but I had the idea and I could follow the sounds.

"I'm more removed from baseball, although Vin Scully paints such a picture I can follow the game. I went to a batting cage once with Eric and stayed about forty-five minutes until I hit one, just so I would know what that felt like."

It was my turn to shake my head. "All right, you did all that so you could understand the games you watch, but you *play* golf. I know what a frustrating monster that game can be, but you play with the big kids—in tournaments."

"Thank God I do. If I didn't, I never would have met Dinah."

I hadn't put that together, but of course it was true.

"Patty is learning the game now. So we go out together, and she lines up my shots for me. Boy, if you don't think *that's* a true test of a marriage! But Patty is great—she doesn't talk a lot—we just enjoy being together. She says 'You play your game, Tom. I'll be your eyes.' There aren't too many people who realize that sometimes you need to be able to do your thing without trying to prove anything."

Again, Tom reached for Dinah, sound asleep by his side. "When this girl came into my life, she gave me a freedom, a sense of aloneness—no relation to loneliness—that is hard for a blind person to come by.

"I can remember days walking to the beach when Dinah and I would literally not have overt communication for an hour or more at a time. The kind of aloneness I'm talking about, I guess, is the right to drift, to have the choice, and not only about where to go; I trusted Dinah's work ethic so much I could daydream my way through the process of getting there. With Nelson, it's conscious work.

"Dinah was also a great golf buddy. My problem always was, when I'd go out on the driving range to practice shots, people would embarrass me. They'd talk out loud: 'Hey, Charlie, do you think he's going to hit it?' "

I could relate to this. When people recognize someone from TV, sometimes they do the same thing. They'll stand right next to you and talk to each other *about* you.

"So Dinah and I would go out to drive balls at midnight," he went on. "What the hell difference did it make to me? I taught Dinah to retrieve the balls by pouring my aftershave on them.

"One night, we got into trouble. At our old house, it was ninety-three yards to the ocean, and forty-one yards to the building next door. It was around one-thirty in the morning, and I thought I could drive a ball *over* the building, but instead I drove it right into this guy's window. When he came steaming out to see what had happened, he recognized me and said, 'Hi, Tom Sullivan, I'm a big fan. I really love your records and your books. That window's going to cost you a hundred and thirty-eight bucks!' "

The day wore comfortably on as we moved from subject to subject.

There was something else I wanted to hear about. "And now you're into tandem bike riding. You really push the marriage-testing business, don't you?"

Tom and Patty had just returned from a tandem bike trip through the Alsace wine country of southern France. I knew they had been planning the trip for over a year to celebrate their twentieth wedding anniversary.

"I had ridden tandem bikes before, but Patty hadn't. Tandem riding is altogether different from riding on a single bike because the balancing and pedaling is really a team effort. As a rule, the larger, stronger person is on the front seat and the smaller one in back. Well, in our case, that was reversed—this small, pretty blond lady was in front, with Lurch bringing up the rear. That throws the weight all wrong and makes takeoffs a little hairy."

When I had heard Patty and Tom were training for this junket, I had had some real misgivings, and I was relieved when they got back home in one piece.

"In the first place, Tom, what made you decide on a tandem bicycle trip?"

Deliberately misunderstanding me, Tom said, "Because I couldn't go wheeling through France by myself!"

A dirty look was totally wasted on my friend, so I just waited for him to continue.

"Patty had never been to Europe. We spent a week on the bike trip and then went on to London and Paris. (I think Patty was training for the shopping finals.) The perfect way to see the wine country is on a bike. You appreciate it so much more. Our guides let us set our own pace. There were eleven couples—some of the group you met at Winter Park—and we'd meet up at various checkpoints during the day."

I had to ask. "Forgive me, Tom. How were you able to enjoy the countryside if you couldn't see it?"

"By the sounds and the smells and the tastes. I keep telling you they were all new. We'd go through these little towns, and I could feel how narrow the streets were and how crooked. In fact, on our map Patty said some were actually designated 'd.c.t.'—'damn cute town!'

"We'd been training for this trip, and we thought we were in good shape. So the very first day we decided to take an optional side trip up to Mont Sainte Odile. Sainte Odile was the patron saint of the blind. The story was that she had been born blind and her father, the Duke, wanted a male heir, so he ordered her killed. Her nurse hid her in a convent. Then, when she was twelve, she was christened and regained her sight! How could we not go there?

"Well, the trip was only fifteen miles, but it climbs two thousand meters. Patty was ready to die. I was so into our breathing and sweating and pedaling and straining that I didn't pay too much attention when Patty said it was too tough; I just kept on—and on. I said all the right husbandly things, like 'Keep pedaling!' Mr. Sensitive, right?

"Finally, Patty couldn't take it anymore. She leaped off the bike and screamed, 'If you want to keep biking, *get a new wife!*' "

Tom told the story with his usual humor, but obviously it had not been so funny at the time.

"That was the first day of our trip. Thank God, things went great for the rest of the time, but I have to say that I rediscovered something I should have learned from Dinah a long time ago. I simply forgot to consider the kind of stress I put the ladies of my life under to enjoy the same pleasures that I do. I wonder how many times Dinah, or even Nelson, might have wanted to yell '*Get a new dog!*' "

I asked about language problems. "You were a little off the beaten track, Tom. Was there much English spoken?"

"Not much English at all. Patty has a little French and I speak German, so we did fine. We weren't far from the German border."

That came as a surprise. "I never knew you spoke German. Chalk up another one for that damn memory of yours. How did it seem not to have Nelson along? You're so used to working with him now, especially on trips."

Tom didn't smile this time. "The seven days were magnificent, but I have to own up to being a little frustrated once in a while. When we'd pull in at the end of the day, I'd still have some residual energy left that I would have liked to work off. If Nelson had been there, we would have gone for a short run. I must say, it made me appreciate the part Nelson plays in terms of my interdependence.

"But I'll tell you when I really wished he'd been there— in Paris. I love the food in Paris and I loved the Left Bank where we stayed, but being dragged from art gallery to art gallery frankly doesn't mean much to me. But Patty goes along with everything I like to do, so it was my turn to do her things.

"We were only there for three days but I gotta tell you: by the third day I was beginning to fray. I knew Patty would have a much better time if I just stayed put somewhere. The Luxembourg park is right there on the Left Bank where we were staying, so on the last day I chose to sit there with a good book while Patty and the others shopped."

"Not the worst place to wait," I said.

"Luxembourg is one of the most beautiful inner-city parks I have ever been in, but what an odd experience it was, Betty. I don't speak French, and though the sounds around me all seemed friendly and people were enjoying the park just as I was, I had the distinct feeling of being trapped. Isn't it strange to feel trapped in all that beauty?"

"What did you do?"

"Understand, I had *chosen* to be in the park, but the feeling of being stuck there, unable to move around, was almost claustrophobic. Boy, did I miss Nelson! Without Nelson's help, my range of mobility was the park bench I was sitting on. And it's funny the tricks your mind plays. I was enjoying my book, but I couldn't concentrate. I started to think things like 'What if something happened to Patty? Could I make myself understood? Could I get back to the hotel?' I knew this was ridiculous and I kept trying to be rational, but was I glad to see my wife when she arrived! She was right on time, too, which isn't always her best thing."

Tom had admitted something I was glad to hear and I couldn't let it go by. "So you missed Nelson? That's a point for our side. Maybe sometimes a vacation is good for everybody. I bet you'll appreciate him more from here on in."

Tom agreed. "Now that I think about it, I should tell him so more often. Funny"—he paused—"but it's tough for me to do that sometimes. Maybe there's some old Porky Sullivan in me someplace. I remember my father could never tell me he loved me. One time, when I was in college, I asked him, 'Dad, why is it so difficult for you to say *I love you?*' He slapped me on the shoulder and said, 'Of course I love you,' as if I should have known it all along."

This time of year, the days were shortening, and while it was only around five-thirty in the afternoon, the room was getting dark. As I got up to turn a couple of lamps on, Tom said, "Where are you going?"

"I'm just putting some light on the subject. I figured it was a symptom when I couldn't see you anymore. It's getting dark in here."

"It looks okay to me." We both chuckled and Tom went on. "That's like one time I was baby-sitting Blythe. We were moving to Cape Cod, and Patty had stayed in Boston to finish up the furniture packing. Blythe cried all night long while I paced the floor holding her in my arms. I thought she just missed her mother, and it wasn't until the next morning that I realized what was wrong—the baby had cried all night because her dumb father had left the lights on."

Timothy and Cricket suddenly exploded as they heard a car pull into the driveway. This time, even Dinah added her voice. It was Eric.

I let him in. He had to wade through two ecstatic small dogs and pay his respects to Dinah before he could make it over to Tom. Eric is a delightful young man. I consider him another of the serendipities of this whole endeavor.

"Well, how did you guys do today?" he asked.

"Fine! God, this woman can ask a lot of questions! Would you believe we're still talking?"

Eric didn't bat an eye. "Oh, yes."

It was hard to believe the day had slipped away from us, but the time had come to pack it in. We made an appointment for Tuesday to cull out some more pictures, and they headed for the car.

Dinah and I stood in the doorway to see them off, but how different it was this time from that first emotional Easter Sunday. Now it was all easy banter and messages for Patty.

"I'll see you on Tuesday then," I said. "I'll think up some more questions."

"Oh, no, you won't. Next time it's my turn." As the car started to roll, Tom leaned out, pointing his finger in my direction—"Next time, I'm going to ask you to tell me about *your* Dinah!"—and they were on their way.

I closed the door, picked up a sweater from the front hall closet, and led the dogs out to the garden where we had started the day.

The earlier breeze had subsided, leaving the air very clear and rather mild. The moon that Tom had never seen was starting on its long climb into the dark sky, and I sat down to wait while the dogs wandered.

I have known my Irish friend too long not to recognize a loaded question when I hear one. "*Your* Dinah," he'd said. That was a first.

Talking about "my Dinah" after four years together means trying to evaluate the impact this Lady has had on my life. It is considerable, and I must be very careful not to oversentimentalize and make her sound larger than life.

Dinah is not some alien being with supercanine powers. She is a very real creature who happens to have been the best—at her job, at her relationships—and who continues to be the best at whatever she puts her heart and mind to. She also exerts a unique influence over people who know her.

Dinah has always had an incredible grasp on what she can and can't do, which continues to serve her in good stead today. Both Tom and I have learned a great deal by her example.

We had been working on this book for a year and a half. (It

wouldn't have taken that long, but for the slight distraction we both call "making a living.") I have become increasingly aware, over that time, that I am a different person from the one who began this project. Tom must realize this, and perhaps the same holds true for him.

When I lost the two people I love the most, my husband and my mother, I found the only reliable sedative for pain was work. As a result, for ten years I have kept my schedule packed as tight as possible. Telling the story of the Leading Lady, however, didn't quite follow the pattern. This time, I didn't choose the job; as you know, it chose me and has never let go. I was truly surprised to find it become the most enjoyable work experience of my life, barely stopping short of obsession.

All through those past ten years, I lived in the present, and if I looked anywhere it was back, never ahead. I was not unhappy; that's just the way it was.

How have I changed?

Now I am looking *forward* to a couple of new writing projects and am already beginning to make notes, even while I am a little sorry to see this one end.

I have acquired a surrogate family from a group of friends.

Unlike ten years ago, this time I am able to accept the fact that my life has entered a whole new stage and will never be quite the same again, because in this case the circumstances are all positive. Dinah is an allegory of passage.

There are changes in Tom as well. He has learned to be more patient, more loving, and less stressed, less wired by his disability, and freer of the need to always prove something. Dinah has helped Tom grow up as she has helped me grow older—which, of course, neither of us has any intention of doing.

Over the course of this endeavor, Patty has received a love letter from her husband, only a small part of which found its way into these pages, Blythe and Sully have found enough good points in an old broad to invite her into the family; and Nelson is finally able to enjoy his time in the limelight.

If we have seemed to overdraw a certain golden retriever and hold her up as the Classic Dog, we have not done the Lady justice. We have simply told you about Dinah and those around her. About Dinah as she is and will always be—someone who has made an indelible impression and a positive difference in the lives she has touched. But aren't those the standards by which all classics are measured?

Although we have seen Dinah from a variety of perspectives, one point of view is still missing. What I wouldn't give to hear from the Lady herself! What were *her* high spots and low moments? What did she learn about *us*? And what could we have done better?

I called Dinah over to speak to her about this. She abandoned her tour of the garden immediately and came to give me her full attention, sitting in front of me eye-to-eye, ears slightly lifted, the perpetual sweet golden retriever smile lighting up her white face. It was a short and admittedly one-sided conversation. The beautiful eyes began to droop; she let her front legs slide and dropped her chin between her paws. The message was loud and clear:

"There you go again! Cluttering the air with all those silly words! When will you learn you can communicate without 'em!" Right again, Dinah.

Sharing these pages has been a joy. Especially so, with the Lady herself stretched at my feet.

Correction. *On* my feet.

ERIC R. WOLD